WADSWORTH PHILOSO

ON

MILLIKAN

Nicholas Shea
University of Oxford

Australia • Canada • Mexico • Singapore • Spain • United Kingdom • United States

COPYRIGHT © 2005 Thomson Wadsworth, a part of The Thomson Corporation. Thomson, the Star logo, and Wadsworth are trademarks used herein under license.

ALL RIGHTS RESERVED. No part of this work covered by the copyright hereon may be reproduced or used in any form or by any means—graphic, electronic, or mechanical, including but not limited to photocopying, recording, taping, Web distribution, information networks, or information storage and retrieval systems—without the written permission of the publisher.

Printed in the United States of America
1 2 3 4 5 6 7   08 07 06 05 04

Printer: Thomson West

ISBN 0-534-60994-5

For more information about our products, contact us at:
Thomson Learning Academic Resource Center
1-800-423-0563

For permission to use material from this text, contact us by:
Phone: 1-800-730-2214
Fax: 1-800-730-2215
Web: http://www.thomsonrights.com

Thomson Higher Education
10 Davis Drive
Belmont, CA 94002-3098
USA

Asia (including India)
Thomson Learning
5 Shenton Way
#01-01 UIC Building
Singapore 068808

Australia/New Zealand
Thomson Learning Australia
102 Dodds Street
Southbank, Victoria 3006
Australia

Canada
Thomson Nelson
1120 Birchmount Road
Toronto, Ontario M1K 5G4
Canada

UK/Europe/Middle East/ Africa
Thomson Learning
High Holborn House
50–51 Bedford Road
London WC1R 4LR
United Kingdom

Latin America
Thomson Learning
Seneca, 53
Colonia Polanco
11560 Mexico
D.F. Mexico

Spain (including Portugal)
Thomson Paraninfo
Calle Magallanes, 25
28015 Madrid, Spain

Contents

Preface

1. **Introduction**
   - 1.1 The Problem of Intentionality 1
   - 1.2 Some Proposals 6

2. **Motivating Millikan's Theory of Intentionality**
   - 2.1 The Source of Millikan's Inspiration 18
   - 2.2 Ideas behind the Theory 21

3. **Teleosemantics: The Theory**
   - 3.1 Language, Thought, and Other Biological Categories 31
   - 3.2 The Launch of LTOBC 41
   - 3.3 Derived Functions 44
   - 3.4 Higher Level Intentionality 50
   - 3.5 Objections and Responses 54

4. **Concepts**
   - 4.1 Introduction: What are Concepts? 62
   - 4.2 Substances 64
   - 4.3 The Place of Substances in Psychology 69
   - 4.4 Against Conceptions 71
   - 4.5 Concepts as Abilities 77
   - 4.6 Substance Concepts through Language 82

5. **Local Natural Information**
   - 5.1 The Relevance of Information 85
   - 5.2 Local Natural Information 87
   - 5.3 Intentionality from Local Natural Information? 89

6. **Externalism** 93

Bibliography 97

Preface

It is no exaggeration to say that Ruth Millikan changed the landscape of philosophy at the end of the twentieth century. Her work is full of originality and exciting insights. It is often challenging and always rewarding. At its best, it offers new ways of thinking about some of the central questions that occur to us as human beings, about our place in nature and how our minds work. There are no simple answers, but Millikan's ideas contain that most valuable prize, the chance of attaining a deeper understanding. As well as important work in the philosophy of psychology, of biology, and of language, she has opened up an entirely new avenue of enquiry in the philosophy of mind. That is, her work on mental content, in which she created a whole new approach to the long-standing and crucially-important problem of how mental representation is possible. This is the area in which she has made the biggest theoretical impact, and for which she is most well-known. Accordingly, nearly two-thirds of this book is dedicated to that issue—Millikan's teleosemantics. Chapter 1 sets up the problem, and chapter 2 explains why Millikan was uniquely well placed to achieve a breakthrough, which is outlined. Chapter 3 fills in the details and answers some objections. There is much more to Millikan's philosophy than teleosemantics, and the book goes on to explain her views in two further areas: chapter 4 introduces her work on concepts and chapter 5 explains her theory of information. These topics fit well with her theory of mental representation since they share some of its central concerns, and help make her teleosemantics clearer by putting it in a wider context. Finally, chapter 6 remarks briefly on a unifying theme—externalism—that runs through Millikan's work.

Millikan's generosity to students is legendary. In my case, she welcomed me out of the blue as a visiting researcher, spent days discussing and explaining her work, and hours working through and commenting on my own. I am also deeply grateful to my PhD supervisor, David Papineau, who has been a model teacher, and a constant source of support in this project. Going through the ideas in this book with him, paragraph by paragraph, has been an invaluable part of my philosophical education. Many thanks to them both.

1
Introduction

1.1 The Problem of Intentionality

Ruth Millikan is engaged in trying to work out how the mind works. It is an enduring puzzle. Modern science has made a lot of progress in explaining why the world is as it is: why it gets dark at night, revealing points of light that move slowly across the sky; how plants grow; where the heat in a fire comes from. But many of the familiar properties of minds remain deeply mysterious. This is especially strange given that we feel we know about our own minds in a much more direct way than we know about any other natural phenomenon. This very familiarity can conceal questions about mental phenomena. One lies in consciousness. At first sight there is nothing more unproblematic than the idea that people are conscious. Yet scientists still haven't managed to discover how consciousness works. Millikan does not tackle consciousness, but she does address an equally pressing question: How do thoughts have meanings? This puzzle is a major, perhaps *the* major, obstacle to discovering how the mind works. Philosophers and scientists over the ages have thought really hard about it without success. In the 1980s, Millikan developed an entirely new

Introduction

approach, which has become an accepted feature of the philosophical landscape. It is called *teleosemantics*. There is much more to Millikan's philosophy than the problem of meaning, but her teleosemantics is the core of a new theoretical perspective on how minds work. So I will start by explaining teleosemantics (in chapters 2 and 3), before exploring some of the other aspects of Millikan's novel way of thinking about thinking. But first I need to say a bit more about the problem of meaning.

The man in the street might doubt the usefulness of this enquiry. Philosophers take something that works in practice and seriously wonder if it works in theory. What is the point of that? Well, it is the theory that will allow us to understand how the mind works. And here we are faced with a phenomenon that is so familiar that it takes a bit of reflection to see the problem.

To focus the issue, let me ask you to engage in a piece of thought. Work out what day of the week it will be in nine days' time. (Did you do it without moving your lips? ... Good.) I have a good guess at your chain of reasoning: *Today is Wednesday, in a week it will be Wednesday again, so two days after that it will be Friday. Friday! Oh good....* My reconstruction is not supposed to capture the words you used—maybe you were talking to yourself, but probably not—but just to describe a series of steps you went through very quickly in your mind. My purpose is not to highlight the series of steps, but to focus on the particular thoughts that make it up, as examples of the sorts of individual thoughts that are constantly arising in our minds. So let's concentrate on the first thought in the chain: that *today is Wednesday*. That thought has a characteristic property: that it can be true or false. If the day you are reading this page (say, January 1, 2004) happens to be a Wednesday, the thought is true. Otherwise, it's false. The thought is not made true by your sincerely believing that 1.1.04 (or whatever day you read this) is a Wednesday, but only by 1.1.04 actually being a Wednesday. This *semantic* property is characteristic of thoughts. Another way of expressing the same point is to say that thoughts are about other things in the world. The thought that dogs are hairy is about dogs and hairiness. Generally, thoughts are picked out by reporting the things they are about: the thought that ... What goes in for "..." serves to pick out the thought in question. For example, "Today is Wednesday" might go into the that-clause. It is called the *content* of the thought.

From the perspective of modern science, thoughts are just physical things in the world. A starting point is to locate thoughts in the head;

but since having a given thought seems to require at least the cooperation of the rest of the body, and perhaps also of bits of the external world, thoughts may be particulars in some larger unit than the brain (e.g., the brain + body, i.e., the person). But still each thought is just some real physical structure, state, event, or process. It is a physical particular. We are used to the idea that physical particulars can have all sorts of properties at once. So, the object I'm sitting on now has the property of being a chair, of being made of wood and leather, of having legs as parts, of being 3 feet high, etc. In just the same way, my thought that *dogs are hairy* is some physical particular with all sorts of properties: it is located inside me, it exists on 1.1.04, it has neurons in my temporal lobes as parts, etc. And there is a further rather interesting property of that same particular: it is about something, namely dogs. So, to understand minds we need to know how on earth it can be that some physical particulars (i.e., human thoughts) can be *about* some other things in the world (i.e., their contents).

The same question can be posed about words. Look at what is found on this page between the following quotation marks: "dog." Think about it as a physical particular. It has lots of properties: it is black ink on white paper, it is less than 1 inch long, in the center is some ink arranged in a circular shape, etc. But it also has more abstract properties: it consists of three letters, it is the word "dog" (i.e., a word of the same type as DOG, Dog, dog, and *dog*—an orthographic type), and it refers to dogs. So marks on a piece of paper can have semantic properties too; they can refer to things and can be formed into complexes (e.g., "dogs are hairy") which are true or false. We can state the conditions under which they are true or false: "dogs are hairy" is true on the condition that dogs really *are* hairy, otherwise it is false. Words and sentences have semantic properties because they are meaningful. In this sense thoughts have meanings too.

There is an easy explanation of how words get their meanings: human thinkers endow them with meaning. English speakers take words of the orthographic type "dog" to refer to dogs. We could have taken words of the type "drogue" to refer to dogs. There is nothing special about the word type that links it with dogs, other than our practices in using it. So it is plausible that the meanings of our words derive from the meanings of the thoughts we express with those words. However, when we go on to ask where the meanings of our thoughts come from, there is no such easy answer.

Thinking about minds runs straight into semantic properties and their puzzling nature. But in looking at other bits of nature, semantic

Introduction

properties are absent. Neither stars nor fires have meanings. So scientists can carry on and explain those phenomena without having to deal with semantic properties. By contrast, the human sphere is permeated with meanings—in our thoughts, interactions, writings, and other creations. Perhaps only humans and their artifacts have semantic properties, or maybe meaningfulness extends further, to other organisms, but it does not extend beyond—streams, rocks, and mountains do not have meanings.

Where do semantic properties come from? Some of the properties studied by scientists are just basic: things just do have mass, or charge. Those properties can be characterized, but it makes no sense to ask how they arise in the first place. Semantic properties don't seem to be like that. Meanings are unlikely to be found in the scientists' final catalog of fundamental particles, forces, properties, and relations. Instead, there is something about thoughts in virtue of which they have the meanings they do. The fundamental properties of bits of humans conspire in just the right way to give rise to semantic properties. On one level of analysis, all that is going on in a person is a complex of biochemical reactions and electrical signals: advanced cookery with switches. The puzzle is how this complex mix can give rise to meanings. We have to ask how it can be that thoughts, as these normal physical particulars, can also bear meanings; how they can refer to things; how they can be true or false. Mental phenomena are shot through with semantic properties, so until we have some clue how meanings arise we face an enormous obstacle to understanding how minds work.

Not everyone agrees, however. Current science explains minds so poorly that even its most basic assumptions can be doubted. There are philosophers who think that semantic properties are fundamental, and that the search for an explanation of how they can arise in nature is misguided. But that is now a minority view. Millikan sees humans as just another animal species and regards her philosophy as continuous with science. In the last four hundred years, science has explained a great variety of previously mysterious phenomena, like lightning, earthquakes, and even life. These phenomena can all be shown to arise from the operation of the fundamental laws of nature. Millikan assumes that semantic properties can be explained in the same way. She therefore shoulders the burden of ensuring that her theorizing is informed by empirical work in psychology and biology, which she does assiduously. The advantage is that her work is of much greater relevance. After all, the majority of people trying hardest to figure out how minds work are scientists. Millikan's assumption that semantic

Introduction

properties are explicable by science ensures that her exciting insights are directly relevant to them.

Within philosophy Millikan's basic assumption is called *naturalism* about semantic properties. (The label derives from a tradition of calling subjects like physics, chemistry, biology, and biochemistry the "natural" sciences.) Naturalism assumes that thoughts are physical particulars forming a normal part of the causal order. They are caused by other thoughts in the brain, and ultimately by the world around us; and they cause actions and other physical happenings. There is no problem about them being causally interrelated with the nonmental in this way, since thoughts are no more than physical particulars. Semantic properties arise out of the ordinary properties that are described by natural science. By now it should be apparent that it is this very perspective which leads to the puzzle: In virtue of what do these physical particulars (biochemical and bioelectrical) have their peculiar semantic properties (meaning, truth, reference)?

Computers provide a good analogy. Internal states of a computer are just physical particulars, typically currents and stored charges in semiconductor circuits. They are caused by physical happenings, like mouse-clicks or the laser light reflected off the tiny bumps on the underside of a CD. Computer states in turn lead to physical effects, like pictures on an LCD screen or ink printed onto paper. Plausibly some of these internal computer states have content; they may be about student numbers (in a database) or chess positions. These computer states interact in ways which are due entirely to their physical properties, but so as to ensure they continue to make semantic sense. Where do their semantic properties come from? The answer seems to stem from our interpreting them, and thus to depend ultimately on the contents of our thoughts. So the meanings of computer states derive from the meanings of human thoughts, as do the meanings of words of natural languages. Computers and words give us a plausible model of how content can attach to physical particulars, but these are cases where that content ultimately derives from the content of human thoughts. Now we need to discover where the underived content of our thoughts comes from.

Almost all of our current understanding of humans depends upon thoughts having semantic properties. In an everyday sense, we are quite good at understanding why people act as they do. Take an example: he went to the kitchen because he wanted something to eat and believed there was food in the kitchen. This reasoning attributes two mental states to the thinker, a desire for food and a belief that there is food in the kitchen. We pick out both thoughts by their semantic properties:

Introduction

what they are about/refer to, that the belief was true, that the desire was satisfied. Such mental states are called propositional attitudes. They are thoughts that are picked out by describing a content, together with the attitude which the thinker bears to that content (belief, desire, fear, etc.). So the belief that dogs are hairy is a propositional attitude. It consists of the attitude *belief* in respect of the content *dogs are hairy*. The contentful part, often found directly after the word "that" in the sentence picking out the thought, is sometimes called a proposition, hence the label "propositional attitude." Mental states that carry these peculiar meaning properties—content, aboutness, reference, truth conditions, satisfaction conditions, etc.—are collectively called *intentional states*. Intentional states should not be confused with what thinkers intend to do. Intentionality is the much broader idea of being directed at the world in the ways we have discussed. Propositional attitudes are paradigm examples of intentional states. Our normal practices in understanding each other depend on picking out intentional states by their contents. That is how understanding minds works in practice. To discover how it works in theory, we need to know how mental states come to have those contents.

If there were an obvious answer to the puzzle, then we could just get on with doing experiments on people and their brains. But all the obvious approaches run into big problems. I will close this chapter by giving an indication of why there are severe difficulties with some apparent solutions to the problem of intentionality. There isn't space to give a thorough philosophical argument against each alternative theory. And there is still no consensus, so one of the rival theories might turn out to be more fruitful than it appears. I simply want to give an indication of why so many philosophers and psychologists felt that research into intentionality had gotten stuck—the field was poised to be enlivened by Millikan's fresh insights.

1.2 Some Proposals

So far, I have pointed to a pervasive feature of human thoughts—that, like words, they have semantic properties. Thoughts are directed onto parts of the environment outside the thinker. They are about something in the world. This *aboutness* brings with it the capacity to *misrepresent*—when the world does not match the thought. And when a thought misrepresents, intuitively there is something wrong with it. So representation and misrepresentation bring a commitment to correctness and incorrectness, which I will call *normativity*. Which is not to make the prescriptive claim that you should not think false thoughts. I use normativity here just to mark the existence of a distinction between correct and incorrect, between true and false. Aboutness, misrepresentation, and normativity: these three features are not really separable, but are just different ways to get a handle on the same underlying phenomenon: *intentionality*. So what we are seeking is an explanation of the intentionality of thoughts. Thus, a good explanation must make clear how thoughts can be about things in the world, how they can sometimes misrepresent, and from where they derive their normativity. And recall that the project here is to seek a naturalistic explanation. Intentionality cannot be taken as basic, but must be seen to arise out of the ordinary properties of natural science.

So intentionality is an interesting and pervasive characteristic of human thoughts. But is it really so puzzling? Isn't there a simple explanation? I want to look briefly at some of the traditional answers and their problems, not to rule them out—it is an area of "blue sky" research and there aren't yet any clear answers that tidy up the field— but just to demonstrate that a convincing explanation cannot be had easily. Ruth Millikan was able to take an entirely new idea and work it up into a promising approach. And the exciting thing about her idea is that it departed radically from the traditional answers, and so served to reshape the landscape of the debate.

(1) Resemblance

Here's a common reaction to the above discussion: my thought that *dogs bite* is about dogs, and not anything else, because it looks like a dog (easy!). The basic idea is that thoughts, or at least some thoughts, are little pictures or images in the mind, and that these images resemble what they are about. So images of dogs represent dogs, etc. Perhaps some of our thoughts abstract away from the pictorial, but their basic aboutness is anchored in looking like a dog, sounding like a bark, feeling like a bite, and so on.

The trouble with this answer is that the intuition that thoughts about dogs resemble dogs is not driven by any resemblance between dogs and DOG thoughts. (I use small capitals for thoughts or concepts, here thoughts of *dogs*.) Rather, the resemblance noticed in introspection is at best between some thoughts about dogs and other thoughts about dogs. So I notice that my memory of a dog is like seeing a dog. But that does not give us the material to break out of the circle of thoughts and into the world. There is no easy sense to be made of what dogs look like in the absence of someone looking at them. Appearances are things in

Introduction

the mind. What makes the visual perception of a dog (its appearance) like a dog (the physical object)? The difficulty is to see how images in the mind can be related to objects in the outside world. So it is very unclear how the intuitive notion of similarity or resemblance of mental images to their objects is to be explicated. There may be some kind of very abstract isomorphism between the structure of thoughts on the one hand, and parts of the world and their structure on the other. That type of answer merits further investigation. But it is a long way from the simple intuition that thoughts are about what they resemble.

Another way to see the problem with the intuitive idea is to unpack the metaphor of resemblance. When we say that a nonmental image (a painting, say) resembles a dog, that is because it produces a similar perceptual experience to that produced by seeing a real dog. That sort of similarity cannot underpin the idea that mental images resemble their referents, on pain of regress. The idea would be that I sit inside my head looking at my thoughts and seeing what they look like. So there is some real *me* that has to deal with my thoughts. It's almost as if there is a little person, a homunculus, sitting inside my head and watching my mental life being displayed on huge screens. One screen is playing my instantaneous perceptions of the world, with accompanying sound, touch, smell, and taste; and other screens are showing my occurrent thoughts, my retrieved memories, reveries, and all the other bits of my current thinking. This shows two problems with the intuitive resemblance idea. The first is that the "inner me" cannot get outside and compare what it sees with actual dogs. All it can judge is that perceptions of dogs are like thoughts of dogs, which are like memories of dogs, and so on. It cannot test for resemblance against the world itself, so it cannot say in what the relation between thoughts and bits of the world consists. The second problem is that we do not have internal homunculi. Our thoughts are not played out to some internal decider and controller—displayed to our minds. Rather, thoughts are constituents of our minds, part of their ongoing processes.

Remember that the project is to give a naturalistic explanation of intentionality. To do so, we need an explanation that goes farther than explaining the intentional properties of one thought in terms of the intentionality of other thoughts (the ones it intuitively resembles). We must have an explanation that is founded in the natural, scientific properties of the thinker (her brain and body) and the world she is in. Of course, such an explanation might prove to be just unavailable. In which case, we might have to add intentionality to our catalog of the basic properties found in nature. And if we did that, then there would be no further objection to explaining the intentionality of one thought by its resemblance to other thoughts whose intentionality is taken for granted. However, that would be to give up before getting started. Even if the project of naturalizing intentionality turns out ultimately to be misguided, in order to give it a proper shot we must avoid explanations that fail to be naturalistic at the very first hurdle.

(2) Causal/Informational

Another straightforward idea is that my DOG thoughts are about dogs because it is *dogs*, in the world, that make me think those thoughts. Lots of theories of content start with this idea—that thoughts are about their causes. However, there are two immediate difficulties. First is how to account for misrepresentation. Take the most basic version of the theory: the content of a person's particular thought DOG is the collection of all the things that have caused thoughts of that type to arise in the mind of that thinker. Now suppose that on one occasion a large muscle-bound cat was glimpsed and caused a DOG thought. According to our toy theory, the content of the thinker's DOG concept will include that cat. Which leaves no room for saying that the thinker misrepresented the cat as being a dog.

The problem gets worse if we were to count as falling under the DOG concept everything that thinker would have applied DOG to, if he had come across it. So suppose that, if I were to visit the Amazon basin and glimpse a tapir through the jungle, I would think it was a large dog. Then the theory says that the content of my DOG thought includes tapirs (or tapirs in those viewing conditions), even if I have never and will never encounter a tapir. The theory ascribes contents on the basis of how we would react to everything we could encounter, whether or not we have, or will, in fact, encounter it. The result is to ascribe contents which are nothing like those we expect, could never be false, and are unlikely to be psychologically explanatory.

A thought's extension is the group of things to which it refers or applies. What the theory needs is some way to narrow down a thought's extension. The extension of a given thought must be narrower than the set of its actual causes, and so must be much narrower than the set of all its potential causes. If so, the thought may misrepresent: something that actually causes the thought may nevertheless fall outside the thought's extension. So the problem for causal theories is to specify what subset of the causes of a thought is to count as part of its content. And the theory must specify this subset in a way which is naturalistic and noncircular. Not an impossible task, you might think. But it has proved

Introduction

difficult to address in any way that is both well-motivated and generally applicable.

The second fundamental challenge faced by causal theories runs just as deep. That is the fact that thoughts, at least in humans, are often caused by other thoughts, not by things in the external world. So thinking about marrowbone makes me think about dogs. Yet these resultant thoughts are not (usually) about other thoughts, but are straightforwardly about things in the world. The causal theorist has to provide a principled account to differentiate occasions when a thought is produced directly by the world, so as to count towards a causal theory of its extension, from occasions when it is caused by other thoughts. This is an especially pressing challenge, given that lots of our thoughts seem to be caused rarely, if at all, directly by the world (think about uranium, say). This second challenge is a subspecies of the first—of delimiting a class of cases in which a thought's causes do fall within its extension. However, it is often neglected, since it is tempting to think of mental states as arising only from our receptivity to the world, and to ask about content in that situation. A convincing causal theory has both to demarcate the perceptual causes, and then delimit that group of perceptual causes that count as content-conferring.

Informational theories of content differ from causal theories, but face similar challenges. A state of affairs carries *information* whenever its occurrence raises the probability of some other state of affairs. For example, smoke carries the information that there is fire nearby, not because of the sure connection of folklore (there's no smoke without fire), but because the occurrence of smoke raises the probability that there is fire nearby. It makes some sense to think that a mental state carries information about that which it represents. So my perceptual belief that *I am seeing a dog* significantly raises the probability that there is a dog in my field of vision. The connection need not be certain, but still the belief carries information about dogs. The hope of informational theories of intentionality is that mental content can be reduced to some restricted class of information. My DOG beliefs do plausibly carry information about dogs, but they carry information about much else besides (e.g., about mammals, about dog tails, and even about my having MARROWBONE thoughts). The challenge for informational theorists is to delineate, amongst all the diverse information carried by a mental state, that which forms part of its content from that which does not. Thus, informational theories must answer the same two broad kinds of challenges levelled at causal theories: to exclude irrelevant external informational links and to exclude informational links to other thoughts. As we saw, these are significant difficulties.

Since there are usually informational connections between a thought and its contents, it cannot be excluded that information will play a role in explaining intentionality. On the other hand, the explanation may go in the other direction—it may be that a good theory of content will explain why contentful states are information-bearing. What is clear is that informational connections cannot do all the work on their own, since there are so many. Most informational relations are clearly not representational, e.g., smoke's connection to fire, or the connection between the color of a chameleon's skin and its background. So to avoid the unattractive conclusion that intentionality is ubiquitous, an informational theory has to say what is special about the information carried by representations. Then it must say why a thought only represents a subset of its possible, statistical causes. Only then is there some prospect of explaining how thoughts have aboutness, and are able to misrepresent.

In short, causal and informational theories of content have mileage left in them, but also have a lot of distance left to cover. They certainly aren't an easy route to naturalizing intentionality.

(3) From Features

One of our worries in the last section was that thoughts are often caused by other thoughts. Indeed, some thoughts seem usually or always to arise that way. Perhaps we can turn that into a virtue. Maybe the content of most of our representations derives from other representations. So perhaps DOG refers to anything that is furry, domesticated, four-legged, medium-sized, and barks, for example. Or, more scientifically, anything that is descended from the first domesticated wolves.

There are broadly two ways in which features could fix content. The most obvious is via definitions, the extension of a representation being all and only those things which satisfy some feature set. A more subtle approach has the set of features as only satisfied approximately, the extension consisting of anything that has enough of the characteristic features. So-called prototype and exemplar theories of concepts pursue the latter approach to representation. But they share with definitional theories a reliance on further features, which themselves represent, as part of the machinery of content determination. For this reason, definitional and prototype theories face some problems in common. For simplicity I will start with the definitional approach,

Introduction

before moving on to say something about prototype theories.

Philosophers are wont to look for definitions. A philosophical practice going back to Plato is to ask "What is X?", then to offer a list of conditions, and then to find counterexamples. So there is a long history in philosophy of attempts to find definitions for terms. These have almost always failed. Granted, these historical cases usually concern difficult and abstract human concepts, like JUSTICE. But recently psychologists and philosophers have tried to formulate definitions for everyday concepts, like DOG and LEMON. They have been spectacularly unsuccessful. The only possible success, out of hundreds of everyday concepts considered, is BACHELOR. Plausibly BACHELOR applies to all and only eligible, unmarried men. But even that is disputed (was Robinson Crusoe a bachelor?).

This is a salutary lesson for theorists of content. A theory of content may sound attractive in its abstract formulation. But it will stand or fall by whether it works well with particular examples. And the definitional theory has done badly on this account. It may still be true, but the lack of good concrete examples, despite extensive investigation, detracts from its empirical plausibility.

Furthermore, since definitional theories define one concept in terms of others, they must deal with the worry that definitions nest within further definitions in an infinite regress. So they usually have some story about how definitions bottom out. The idea is that there is some class of thoughts (perceptual representations) that achieve their intentionality some other way, and that definitions ultimately terminate there. They still need some theory of the intentionality of these definitional primitives. Another way to go is to allow terms to be interdefined. So when the features in the definition of a concept have their definitions spelled out in terms of further features, and so on, the process is permitted to arrive back at the original concept being defined. Proponents argue that the permitted circularity is not fatal. The picture is of some complex web of interrelated definitionally connected concepts, where the complex of definitional connections matches the real connections between things and their properties in the world. The difficulty is to see how this web can help to naturalize intentionality.

Definitional theories are a subspecies of inferential role theories of content. Inferential role theories rely upon the inferences in which a concept figures to determine its content. Definitions underpin one species of inference: we infer from (1) Tom is unmarried; and (2) Tom is male; to (3) Tom is a bachelor; and we may make that inference because of the definition of BACHELOR. Inferential role theories can allow connections other than those which are definitive of some concept to be determinative of content. So we may infer from (4) Tom is a bachelor; to (5) Tom is under 40. That inference is not certain, but is still pretty reliable. It does not follow from any definition of BACHELOR. Inferential role theories can allow such inferences also to play a role in content determination.

The first challenge for such theories is to say whether all the inferences in which a concept figures (or might figure) count as determinative of reference. The problem of distinguishing the content-determining inferential roles is a direct analogue of the objection to causal/informational theories that we saw in the last section, namely that too many things in the world are causally or informationally connected to a given thought for causal or informational connections alone to be determinative of content. With inferential roles, the analogous problem is that typical thoughts have too many inferential roles. So my DOG thoughts are inferentially connected not only to furriness and barking, but also to the name "Penny" (my childhood pet), and to old-fashioned wind-up gramophone players. Perhaps all of these connections contribute to the content of my DOG thoughts: content holism. But then my thought is not the same as anyone else's, and its content changes every time one of my beliefs changes. Nor is it clear that thoughts will ever misrepresent, since everything I actually apply my thought to in virtue of an inferential connection will thereby fall in its extension. Thus, a theorist employing inferential roles needs a principled way of distinguishing the inferential roles that are to count towards content determination from those that are not. Some philosophers think there are "canonical" conditions in which a thought is formed. It's hard to see what such preferential conditions could be since, given the diversity of contexts in which we do our thinking, any thought may be connected, more or less, to any other one. I used the example of dogs and gramophones, but given a bit of ingenuity you can think up a context in which there is an inferential connection between any two thoughts at all. Go on, give it a try. Pick two contents at random, and let your imagination roam! So the challenge is to explain why some of this plethora of inferences count as content-determinative, when most do not. It is pretty difficult to find an appropriate principled distinction; influential philosophical work by Willard Quine in the mid-twentieth century argues that the task is hopeless—he gives us reasons to think that no such distinction can ever be drawn (see section 4.4 below).

Inferential role theories also face the problem of regress, which we

Introduction

saw arose for definitional theories. Thus, inferential role theories are usually applied only to a subcategory of thoughts. Other thoughts are taken to be basic, and to derive their intentionality in another way. Often relatively primitive perceptual experiences, like the sight of a patch of red color directly ahead, are held to have some causal /informational content. These perceptual primitives are then used to define more and more complex concepts, until arriving at everyday thoughts about dogs. But that approach requires two theories of content, one for the perceptual primitives and one for the concepts found at roughly the lexical level (DOG, etc.). If there is a good theory of intentionality available for perceptual primitives, why won't it work for lexical-level concepts too? As with definitions, the alternative is to accept some circularity, allowing thoughts to be interdefined; and then to argue that the way a set of thoughts interrelate matches the way that individuals and properties in the world interrelate. The idea is that we have a sufficiently rich network of interconnecting ideas that there is only one way that the world can be mapped onto them. Such theorists have difficulty accounting, on the one hand for the uniqueness of the supposed mapping, and on the other for misrepresentation. Misrepresentation is hard to account for because, as we have seen, some of the connections between thoughts (inferences) will be wrong, and so should not be determinative of content.

Definitions seek to set out a set of conditions which items in the extension of a concept must satisfy, called necessary and sufficient conditions. Prototype theories drop the requirement for necessary and sufficient conditions, and instead hold that content is determined by a set of statistically associated features. Prototype theories are the other major type of theory in which features are determinative of content. Such theories can ascribe plausible contents to everyday concepts, but have problems of their own. In particular, it is not clear how they deal with conceptual combination. Furthermore, to avoid regress, their sets of features should terminate with some primitive concepts, which refer in some other way. And as with all inferential role theories, prototype theories must answer the charge that the contents they ascribe are too fine-grained: that they are incommensurable between individuals and change often in the lifetime of an individual.

In sum, theories of content that rely upon interrelations between contentful states do not yet provide a naturalistic explanation of intentionality.

(4) Instrumental

All these problems with explaining the content of mental states! And yet we are all perfectly able to ascribe contents to our own thoughts and the thoughts of others. Indeed, we partly judge a theory of content against our preexisting intuitions about what the contents of various thoughts are. This seems to be another case of taking something that works in practice and seriously wondering whether it works in principle. Perhaps all we need is the practice. So here's a basic theory of content: the content of a person's mental states is that content which ordinary observers of that person would ascribe to his mental states. And implicitly, that's all there is to it.

At first sight this is an attractive suggestion. It takes some further work to refine the story to deal with difficult cases, and to take account of self-ascription of contents. But it can be worked up into a theory that intuitively gets the right results, as you would expect. Nor need the theory be unnaturalistic. People's practices in ascribing contents are a perfectly natural part of the causal order. No basic intentional states are postulated to which the ascriptions must answer. The theory can simply rely upon ascriptive practices as constitutive of content.

This sort of "theory" of content does not really engage with our project. We are assuming that individual mental states (tokens) can be identified prior to asking what content they have (i.e., what mental-state type they fall under). Instrumentalist theories just individuate mental states by their mental types (including their contents). So they are not addressing the question to which we are seeking a naturalistic answer: What are the non-semantic properties of a mental-state token that give it the content it has?

Instrumentalist theories of content can make a valuable contribution in clarifying our concepts of aboutness, representation, misrepresentation, etc. This is a relatively *a priori* exercise (philosophers can do it from their armchairs). Naturalistic theories of content go further—they attempt to uncover the deeper structure of the phenomenon which the instrumentalist has described. Millikan's teleosemantic theory is an example. An analogy can be made with two ways of getting to understand the concept WATER. The armchair approach is to consider the kinds of beliefs we are committed to about water: that it is liquid, colorless, odorless, potable, etc. This is a valuable exercise, but differs from what the scientist aims at: to discover the underlying nature of water. Through experiments it was discovered that water consists of collections of the simple molecule

Introduction

H₂O, weakly joined by hydrogen bonds to form a liquid. Science can explain how that molecule gives rise to the observable properties found in the everyday characterization of water. The instrumentalist approach to intentionality is more like the project of properly describing the everyday concept of water: an important contribution, but not aimed at finding the deeper nature of the phenomenon in question.

As such, instrumental theories of content do not feel very explanatory. We were looking for some underlying properties of mental states to account for their bearing the contents they do, in order to understand why content attributions are such a powerful way to predict and explain behavior. These theories say content is just whatever predicts and explains behavior, and that there need be no further basis for its explanatory utility. Of course, that may be right. But before we give up and adopt such an instrumentalist theory about content, we should look pretty hard to check that no other options provide more satisfying explanations.

(5) God

Here's another way to account for the intentionality of human mental states: it derives from some divine power. My DOG thoughts are about *dogs* because that is what God intends they should refer to. This would give a good explanation of intentionality: thoughts are about what they are designed to represent. They misrepresent just in case we fallible mortals misapply them to things other than the things they are supposed to stand for. And the normativity derives from God. This theory is offered lightly. But it illustrates a point. The theory fails entirely to be naturalistic since it imports purposes and design based on the purposes of an omniscient designer. But perhaps the urge to explain intentionality by means of design and purposes is a clue. A naturalistic theory of content can only do so if it can naturalize design and purpose. And that is where we will look next.

Proposal	Difficulties
(1) Resemblance	(i) What is resemblance (between mental item and external object)? (ii) Homuncular?
(2) Causal/informational	(i) How to delineate content-determinative causes/links? (ii) How to exclude other thoughts as content determinative?
(3) Inferential role	(i) Circularity, or needs a separate theory of content for primitives (ii) Delimiting the content-determining inferences or accepting holism
(4) Instrumental	Explanatory?
(5) God	Not a naturalistic account of purposes

Fig. 1 Some Basic Proposals for Naturalizing Intentionality

2
Motivating Millikan's Theory of Intentionality

2.1 The Source of Millikan's Inspiration

So far, we have seen that there is a deep puzzle about the intentionality of human thoughts. The problem is to account for their aboutness, normativity, and capacity for misrepresentation. We canvassed some traditional answers and saw why they each come up against difficulties. By the early 1980s, philosophers agreed that this was one of the most important questions facing naturalistic philosophy of mind, and many thought too that some new approach was needed. So, where to look next?

Often it takes something unexpected to break an impasse: a new perspective, a different approach, or a creative leap. Ruth Millikan was in a position to make this leap. She started with the essential core skills: academic training and an enquiring and analytic mind. Following a science-based degree at Oberlin, she took a PhD in philosophy at Yale, where she acquired a deep historical knowledge of the subject. That has allowed her to see problems in a broader context than the intensity of currently-fashionable debates allows. Wilfred Sellars was an influential supervisor, reflected in Millikan's abiding commitment to empiricism in the philosophy of mind. However, her graduate school background does not distinguish her from most leading academic philosophers. It was three extra ingredients that gave her the chance to create a whole new approach.

The first is her creativity. This shows itself in her willingness to pursue a line of enquiry for its interest, without getting stopped at the outset by potential criticisms. Millikan approaches other people's ideas with an open mind. She is willing to take an idea to see where it can lead, rather than criticizing it out of existence with academic bravura. Analysis, criticism, and working out the details come later; the starting point is to create some new material to work on, and in that process the strange and unorthodox are more valuable than the accepted views.

Millikan's second asset is her love of the natural world. She is fascinated by how things work, in a practical sense. Not for her the life of an ivory-tower professor who can't change a fuse. She will not only fix the plug, but make use of the attached power drill to build a dock for her boat. As a child, she passed long summers at the family cabin on an island in the Voyageurs National Park, in the remote borderlands of Northern Minnesota. Without electricity, TV, or telephone, not only were practical skills at a premium, but the main entertainment was interacting with the natural world. So from an early age Millikan has been fascinated with the living world and how it works. Indeed, she still lives in the woods, with deer in her garden, and takes off in the summer for the same cabin in the wilds.

The more you understand animals and plants, the more complexity you find. And all this fine design was arrived at by the mindless forces of natural selection. Millikan was especially well-placed to appreciate just how much clever intricacy may be explained by natural selection. That doubtless predisposed her to thinking about whether the complexity of human cognition might be explained in a similar way, an idea that was unorthodox at the time, bordering on the heretical. Darwinian ideas are often associated with right-wing politics and run against the current of the liberal-left academic establishment. Perhaps these ideas were also perceived to be tainted after their famous misappropriation by the Nazis. This may be why it took until the 1970s for biologists and philosophers of biology to realize that the concept of function employed in biology should be explained in Darwinian terms. Until then it had been assumed that functional explanation was based in current organization, or somehow depended upon the effects that a trait would give rise to (bizarrely: to explain how things are now on the basis of what effects they will bring about in the future). Nor was it until the 1970s that evolutionary accounts of human behavior became widely accepted—by focusing on universal human traits researchers were able to side-step previous objectionable attempts to investigate supposed genetic differences between "races." But still it took some academic bravery for Millikan to take up these Darwinian ideas within mainstream philosophy.

So Millikan brought to the subject a detailed understanding of the living world and the creative ability to pursue new and unfashionable ideas. These were important sources of her new theory. The third special ingredient was to develop her ideas in relative isolation. Promising new ideas are often destroyed before they have developed the strength and coherence to withstand criticism. Academics survive on their reputations, and it is much easier to appear clever with well-directed criticism than by defending unfamiliar new ideas. So there is a bias in the academic establishment favoring criticism over creativity. Of course, intelligent critical analysis is one of the most important skills that philosophers can bring to a theory, in any area of enquiry. However, applied too soon it is an eroding flood that can undermine a good idea before the foundations are consolidated. Millikan's circumstances allowed her to develop her ideas away from the mainstream, building them up over time into a coherent and well-supported theory before having to face her critics.

This isolation was an indirect result of the need to combine her work with bringing up a family. She graduated at a time when it was still unusual for women to pursue a career in philosophy. But she was undeterred. In her family, learning had been highly valued for generations, and the women had been as scholarly as the men. Her mother was an academic pioneer, breaking into the male world of geology as the first woman PhD in her department. Her paternal grandmother was a self-taught proponent of Darwinism. This formidable woman stares out of a portrait in Millikan's office with a bold intelligence which contrasts markedly with her staid dress. Her son, Millikan's father, a Rhodes scholar and a professor of physics, was another important influence. But Millikan still faced the perennial problems of combining work with bringing up children. She supported her family by juggling home life with part-time philosophy teaching at the University of Connecticut (UConn). And at the same time she managed to pursue her research, working largely in isolation, but with moral support from her husband, an experimental psychologist. Philosophical success often goes to those at the famous institutions.

Undeterred, Millikan persevered determinedly as a part-time assistant professor at a rural state university. In fact, long after her theory received international acclaim, UConn's most famous philosopher remained untenured. The university was spurred into resolving the anomaly when distinguished departments started trying to tempt Millikan away. She remained loyal and accepted a titular chair at UConn.

These very difficulties in the early years allowed her theory to flourish. She was able to take her original ideas and develop them on her own into a comprehensive and coherent theory. That took sheer hard work. But it produced a structure that, by the time it was picked over by her peers, could withstand their criticism.

So Millikan had three distinctive advantages in addressing the long-standing problem of naturalizing intentionality. Unusual creativity and open-mindedness allowed her to generate new ideas. Her interest in how things work, deep knowledge of the natural world, and scientific outlook gave her a rich source for those new ideas. And her relative academic isolation gave her the chance to develop those ideas fully before they could be critically demolished.

In the next section, I will motivate the basic idea of her theory of intentionality, before going into some of the fascinating details in the next chapter.

2.2 Ideas behind the Theory

In the last chapter, I hinted at deriving intentionality from the idea that representations are *supposed* to represent certain things. They are about what they are supposed to represent. That is the way that the intentionality of words on the printed page derives from our purposes as readers. I suggested that the intentionality of thoughts could similarly derive from God's purposes—from what He designed them to represent. That would not be the naturalistic theory we are after, but the observation leads to an interesting historical parallel. Before Darwin, it was widely believed that the intricacy of design in nature was created by God, each design for its own purpose. That way of thinking left no problem with understanding why feet are for walking; it is because feet were made for walking. Since Darwin we can see how there can be purposes even in the absence of a Creator. According to the theory of evolution by natural selection, an undirected thoughtless process can lead to organisms that are designed to perform certain functions. Of course, organisms are not designed in exactly the same way that a

Motivation

human engineer designs things. But Darwinism retains the essential feature of a designed system—there is something that it is supposed to do, and if it fails, then it is malfunctioning. So evolution by natural selection can step into the role that God once played in explaining purposes in nature. But if divine purposes provide a potential explanation of the phenomenon we are considering, intentionality, perhaps Darwinism can replace God in that explanation too to give us a naturalistic theory of intentionality. The hope is that as natural selection can form the basis of the normativity of biological functions, it can also underpin the normativity of intentionality.

To pursue this suggestion, let's start by seeing how natural selection explains the normativity of biological functions (recall that this is not evaluative or prescriptive normativity, but just existence of a distinction between well-functioning and malfunctioning). An example of artificial selection illustrates the approach. I want to get my family across a small mountain torrent. I try out several logs to act as a bridge. Some break, some don't reach, and others are too wobbly. Finally I choose the most solid one and lead the children across. The function of the log is then to form a bridge, and to be strong and stable. That is what it was selected for. The same applies when humans selectively breed domestic animals. Greyhounds emerged from breeding dogs for speed, at each generation breeding only from the fastest offspring. What then is the purpose of the greyhound's long legs? To enable it to run fast, because that is what they were selected for. Had greyhounds instead been bred in order to span wide gaps, then their long legs would have had that different function. Darwin's insight was that a process like artificial selection takes place blindly in nature. When organisms reproduce the offspring vary. Not all offspring survive to reproduce in their turn, and the variations can alter their chances of survival. When a variation arises that does lead to more offspring, the result is that it has been preferentially copied into the next generation. These are the two key features of evolution by natural selection: descent and modification. In nature the modifications occur at random, because of sexual recombination and because of tiny errors that are occasionally introduced when the genome is copied into a new generation. And unlike a dog breeder, nature selects blindly. The organisms that survive are those that happen to reproduce more; which is in turn affected by how they function.

To see how this process can lead to a normative distinction between function and malfunction, consider an organ like a lion's heart. There are lots of things it does: contracts regularly, pumps blood, and makes a characteristic beating noise. Yet not just anything an organ does forms one of its functions. A lion's heart makes a tasty meal, but that is not one of its functions. Making a rhythmic sound is not part of the purpose of a heart, either. Darwinism explains why. It starts by asking why there are hearts around today. The answer is partly due to the way that hearts functioned in the past, in the bodies of ancestors of today's lions. These ancestral hearts contributed to the job of keeping past lions alive. It is because past lions were kept alive that they were able to reproduce, and thus produce the lions we see today, with hearts of their own. So the functioning of ancestral lion hearts partly explains why there are hearts around today. Out of all the things that a lion's heart actually does, and all the things it could potentially do, its biological functions are those things that it did in the past that contributed to the survival and reproduction of those ancestral lions. Thus Darwinism explains why pumping blood is a function of lion hearts, and why making beating noises is not. Furthermore, it gives us a notion of malfunction. When a lion is born with a heart with a leaky mitral valve, that heart is no longer doing something that accounts for past success. When mitral valves leaked in the past, the lion did not go on to reproduce (as often). So leaky hearts are malfunctioning. Thus, evolution by natural selection gives us a principled way of saying what are *the* functions of any evolved trait. And in doing so it gives us a normative notion of malfunction. That is, it gives us a sense in which a norm has been breached when a trait does not perform its evolved functions.

So far, so good; but this explanation does not carry over directly to representations. If intentionality were just a matter of biological function then intentionality would pervade every aspect of the living world. Every living organism is packed full of traits with biological functions, from the protein coat of a virus particle to the delicate structure of the human eye. Most of these traits lack intentionality. Neither the virus coat nor the human eye is *about* anything. They may function or malfunction, but there is no sense in which they can be false. Intentionality is a feature of only those traits with a very special sort of function: a function involving representation. That gives us an outline: biological functions derive their normativity from natural selection, and intentionality arises in a small subclass of biological functions, namely those traits that have the biological function of representing something. So the remaining task is to explain what it is to represent. Sadly, that question is not a great advance on the initial problem of explaining intentionality. We have succeeded in reformulating the problem in

Motivation

different terms, but we are left with the crucially difficult task of elucidating what is distinctive of representation. The new outlook gives hope, because it suggests that the right approach is to look for intentionality in nature, and then to discern what is distinctive of it, considered in the light of biological functions. If representation can be adequately characterized as a biological function, then Darwinism will provide a source of normativity. Otherwise, natural selection just remains a promising analogy.

To address such a difficult task it helps to start with the easiest possible examples. So Millikan looked for intentionality in simpler cases than human cognition. Nature provides a rich source of examples. For, although not every evolved trait has intentionality, there are lots of traits in other animals that look as though they might. Millikan's nature-loving background gave her a good stock of examples to think about. The strategy is to find a class of natural traits that are plausibly intentional, and to use those examples to determine what distinguishes intentionality from other biological functions.

One good example springs from Millikan's childhood summers on the northern lakes: beavers. Beavers signal danger by splashing their tail on the water. Other beavers respond to this splash by diving underwater, often returning to their lodge via its protected underwater entrance. This splashing behavior has a biological function—to avoid predators. But the splash itself also seems to be about something: danger. If it is produced when there is no danger then something has gone wrong: the splash says there is danger when there isn't, so it says something false.

Other animals have much more complex signalling systems. Honeybees are a favorite Millikan example. Bee dances have become one of her trademarks. In a photograph of Millikan in front of the giant honeybee exhibit at the New York Science Museum, she seems to acknowledge this with an ironic smile. It is now well-known that bees perform a complex dance inside the hive to signal to other bees the location of a source of nectar. That was originally a startling discovery. At first people refused to believe that one bee could "tell" another where to find honey, "representing" in a dance the direction and distance of groups of flowers. But the evidence built up. Bees returning to the hive don't dance at random. Rather, they waggle to and fro along a straight line. The direction of that line corresponds systematically with the direction of the flowers they have just visited. In addition, the number of waggles they make along the line corresponds with how long it takes to get to the flowers, and the vigor of the dance varies with the desirability of the food source. These correlations are already impressive, but the knockout finding is that bees watching a dance behave in a systematic way (since it is dark inside the hive, the "watching" is done entirely by touch). They fly in the direction indicated by the main axis, and keep flying for the amount of time indicated by the number of waggles they observe (this description is slightly simplified, but the details affect the validity of the example). These observations together provide compelling evidence that bee dances do indeed signal the location of nectar. For Millikan this discovery was an important addition to her armory of examples because it acts as an intermediary between the blind purposes of biofunctions and the complexities of representation. On the one hand, bee dances do seem to be representational. On the other hand, bees are relatively simple creatures, making it unquestionable that their traits can be explained in terms of evolution by natural selection. Philosophers might suspect that something special and *sui generis* is needed to explain the intentionality of thought, but no such case could be made for the bees' representations.

Millikan's task was to discern what constitutes the difference between intentionality and other kinds of natural functions. The two examples of the beaver splash and the bee dance illustrate the features that underpin this distinction. They are useful examples because the representations are out in the open, produced by one organism and used by another. This structure is not so apparent when considering internal representations. Millikan's insight was to observe that representational systems are always divided up into a representation, a system that produces that representation, and a system that uses that representation in order to perform some further function. In bees, the dances are the representations. Bees have a system that uses those representations to fly to flowers. Millikan calls the system that makes the representations the "producer," and the system that makes use of them the "consumer." In bees, the consuming system sees the dance of another bee and ensures the watching bee flies a certain distance in a given direction as a result. The function of the whole representational system is to take the bees to nectar. That is divided into two subfunctions. The producer's function is to produce a dance that corresponds to the location of nectar. The consumer's function is to take the bee to the location indicated by the dance. A particular dance mediates between these two systems. It acts as a representation that signals to the consuming system the location of nectar, as indicated by the producing system.

The same articulation into a producing system and a consuming system can be seen in the beaver's splashing behavior. The function of

Motivation

the whole setup is to keep beavers away from danger. The consumer mechanism contributes by taking the beaver to safety when it hears a splash. The producer mechanism contributes by making a splash when danger is observed. The splash itself sits in between producer and consumer, acting as a representation of danger. To apply this thinking to mental representation, Millikan will divide the internal processes involving representations into a system that produces representations and a cooperating system that consumes them. But, unlike the beaver and honeybee cases, both these systems will be inside the same thinker, so that the intermediate representations will also be internal.

Do these natural representations, the bee dance and the beaver splash, really admit of misrepresentation? A representational system can go wrong in several ways. Something might fail in the consuming system. For example, a beaver might hear a splash but fail to take cover. Alternatively, there may be something wrong with a given representation. Think of a splash that is produced in the absence of danger. The splash represents danger and the beavers dive, but there is in fact no danger around. In that case, Millikan argues, the splash is false: it means *danger here now,* but there is none. The same applies to the bees. A consumer bee can fail to follow the directions in the dance it has seen. It could be blown off-course, or run out of energy before it arrives. However, the dance production-consumption system can also fail to lead the consumer bee to nectar for a different reason: because the dance represents the wrong location. Suppose the dancing bee makes the wrong number of waggles, or gets disoriented and dances in the wrong direction. Then there will be no nectar in the direction indicated. The dance represents *nectar at distance r in direction θ* when there is none at (r,θ). Millikan argues that in such a case the dance is literally false.

So Millikan saw that representing is not a function of a single undifferentiated system. Instead, representation takes place in a system composed of a producer and a consumer, with representations as intermediates produced by one and used by the other in order that the entire system should perform in the way natural selection designed it to. In the bee and the beaver, the producer and consumer systems operate in different organisms, but more typically the systems will lie within the same organism and the intermediate representations will be internal. The same distinction applies in both cases. This distinction allows her to focus on the important role of the consuming mechanism in determining the content of the intermediate representations—what I will call a "forward-looking" approach to content. Natural selection cares only about results, so biofunctions must depend ultimately upon a system's effects, not upon what causes it to behave as it does. Others have tried to make progress with the idea that it is a function of a representation to indicate, covary with, or carry information about some external state of affairs. This idea cannot stand alone, since looking at the circumstances in which representations are produced does not connect with their effects. Millikan's forward-looking theory surmounts this problem by explaining what it is to have the function of detecting or indicating some external state of affairs in terms of the functions of the consumer mechanism.

The importance of the forward-looking approach can be seen in some real-life experimental research. The visual system of the frog was studied in the 1950s. Ganglion cells were discovered in the retina, very early in visual processing, that respond selectively to little black dots moving across the frog's visual field. Lots of objects and patterns were presented to the frog's eye, but this particular cell only fires strongly when a black pellet (say, on the end of a thin piece of wire) is moved in front of the eye. None of the other patterns caused this cell to respond. It was surprising to discover such responsiveness to a higher-level feature of the scene presented, rather than a basic visual attribute. There is then a question about the function of these cells. Are they extracting information about movement to be used in later processing, or are they themselves representing something? The question was answered when it was observed that these cells trigger the frog's fly-catching reflex. Activity in these cells is enough on its own to trigger the mechanism by which the frog darts its tongue out in the direction of the moving pellet. This reflex is stimulated even if the cells are artificially activated by applying an electric current. The tongue reflex is produced as surely as, in eighteenth-century experiments with electricity, applying an electric current to a frog's leg made it contract. So researchers were able to conclude that these ganglion cells represent the presence of a fly (or more precisely, some flying suitable prey). That is a commonsense conclusion. However, notice that it relies on the strategy that Millikan subsequently made explicit: to look to the consumption mechanism in determining the content of a representation. And this is a case, unlike the bee dance and the beaver splash, the representation is an internal state mediating between an internal-producer subsystem and an internal-consumer subsystem. The 1950s researchers adopted the forward-looking approach to work out what these internal cell-firings meant. Millikan's theory endorses this forward-looking approach generally, both for external representations like the bee dance and beaver splash,

Motivation

and for internal representations like the frog's fly-detector cells. In the internal case the theory requires some internal subsystem that, in order to perform its function, consumes the representations.

Producer	Representation	Consumer
Beaver that splashes its tail on detecting danger	Tail splash	Other beavers: dive underwater
Bee that dances on returning from nectar	Bee's dance	Other bees: fly in the direction & for the distance indicated
Frog's eye and optical system	Firing in a retinal ganglion cell	Tongue-dart mechanism in the same frog

Fig. 2 Producer, Representation, and Consumer

In summary, the content of a representation depends crucially upon what the system consuming it takes it to represent. But beware. That cannot be a final answer, since it still makes an unexplained use of "represent," which is the phenomenon we set out to explain in naturalistic terms. We have seen the problems with talking loosely: the content of a representation is X if the function of that representation is *to represent* X. How do we adapt this in the light of the idea that we must look forward, to consumers, as determinative of content? Here is a first try: the content of a representation is X if the consumer mechanism (when well-functioning) takes it to represent X. But then we still have the unexplained use of "represent." How to eliminate it? Millikan had an insight about that too. Her idea is that what a representation stands for cannot be found in the function of any system, but instead in the conditions in the world that must be in place if the system is to function as designed.

Consider again the bee dance. It is performed on a vertical wall inside the hive. The angle of the main axis of the dance from vertical is interpreted by the consumer mechanism (in other bees) as representing the angle between the direction of the food source and the sun. The

Motivation

observers are caused to travel in that direction, and to travel a distance that is a mathematical function of the number of waggles observed. Suppose the bee dances n waggles in a line at angle θ to the vertical. The mathematical transformation performed by the consuming system causes the bee to fly r feet in direction θ from the sun. Provided the consumer system calculates the mathematical transformation as it was designed to, the consumer system will be well-functioning. That is, it will be functioning in the same way as accounted for the past successful operation of the mechanism (which in turn led to reproduction of more bees, and hence of more copies of the mechanism). However, well-functioning does not guarantee success. Success requires that there really is nectar r feet away in direction θ. That is a condition for the successful performance of the mechanism's function. The consumption system can only succeed in functioning as designed if there is nectar at (r, θ). This condition for the normal performance of the consumer's function is the same as the content of the representation: that *there is nectar at (r, θ)*. Therefore, Millikan says (roughly) that the content of a representation is found in the normal conditions for the performance of the function of the mechanism that consumes it. Among those conditions are many common background requirements, such as sufficient nutrition, being at the right temperature, etc. But some condition is specific to the consumer's function in relation to a specific representation. That condition is the content of that representation.

This idea also works for internal representations. Many bacteria in lakes and oceans display *magnetotaxis*: they swim in the direction of lines of magnetic flux. In the Northern Hemisphere they swim towards magnetic north. This is achieved by means of microscopic particles of a magnetic mineral enclosed within a membrane inside the bacterium, called a *magnetosome*. The local magnetic field acts on the magnetosome and rotates the whole bacterium towards magnetic north. The bacterium's constant forward-swimming motions then take it in that direction. In the Northern Hemisphere, the magnetic field not only points towards northwards, but also broadly downwards, since lines of magnetic flux descend into the earth. (Compasses are designed to compensate for this downwards force, so that the needle points north horizontally—which is why Northern-Hemisphere compasses perform badly south of the equator.) The effect of this simple connection between magnetosome and swimming is that the bacteria stay away from the oxygen-rich water at the surface of the sea, which is toxic. The swimming mechanism was designed to function by taking the organism

Motivation

in the direction indicated by the magnetosome. However, it is a condition for the normal performance of that function that that is the direction of oxygen-depleted water. That is, the magnetosome-to-swimming mechanism functioned successfully in the past, causing the reproduction of the bacterium and hence of the mechanism itself, only when the magnetosome pointed in the direction of oxygen-depleted water. That is the condition for successful performance of its function. Hence, the orientation of the magnetosome represents the direction of oxygen-depleted water. That is what it is *about*. And when the magnetosome points at oxygen-rich water (deflected, say, by a passing ship) it does something *wrong* and says something *false*. So we have aboutness, normativity, and the capacity for misrepresentation. In short: intentionality.

This chapter has sketched the general idea behind Millikan's theory. Worries remain about whether it delivers the necessary level of determinacy for the content it describes. For example, why does the bacterium represent oxygen-free water rather than magnetic north? Why is the frog visual system representing flies rather than little black dots? We will see in the next chapter that Millikan's teleosemantics does deliver the desired amount of determinacy. The purpose of this chapter was to highlight two of the insights that primed her theory for success: first, the forward-orientation towards representation consumers as determinative of content; and second, the focus on conditions for successful performance of the consumer's function. However, a useful theory needs more than some insights and good examples. It can only be assessed when it is worked out in detail. That is what Millikan did, painstakingly and at length, in her seminal book *Language, Thought, and Other Biological Categories* (1984), "LTOBC" for short. In many philosophical theories, "the devil is in the details"—the details are philosophically important, differentiating a theory that makes sense from one which merely sounds attractive. The next chapter examines a few of the details that are particularly interesting, and in doing so gives an idea of what Millikan's theory looks like when it is fully worked out. It also tells the story of the launch of Millikan's theory onto an unsuspecting philosophical community.

3
Teleosemantics: The Theory

3.1 Language, Thought, and Other Biological Categories

Millikan's theory of intentionality is set out in her first book, *Language, Thought, and Other Biological Categories* ("LTOBC"), published in 1984. The theory is often called teleosemantics (from *semantics*—the study of meaning—and *teleo-*, meaning purpose). In Millikan's case the purposes derive from biological functions and the purposes of natural selection, so she has also called her theory biosemantics. Of course, there is not scope in an introductory book to recapitulate the complexity of Millikan's theory. The ultimate source must be LTOBC itself. This chapter can only be an introduction. It serves two purposes. First, it will illustrate some interesting features of the worked-out theory. Second, it will provide an overview that can act as a guide to the territory. LTOBC is a hard book, worthy of careful study, and a rough map of the theory will come in handy for those who read it. In addition, having surveyed the theory I will tell the story of its release. This will give an idea of the excitement Millikan produced when she launched LTOBC on the community of academic

The Theory

philosophers and psychologists.

Millikan provocatively calls language and thought "biological" categories because she explains intentionality in terms of evolutionary functions. However, she does not mean to adopt wholesale the theories of biology. She feels herself free to define her own concepts with which to elaborate the theory. Nor does she rely exclusively on common-sense intuitions about organisms' traits and their functions. Rather, she constructs an entirely new theory, going to great lengths to explain what she means by each of her terms before making use of it. As with scientific theories, the concepts deployed need not match our everyday concepts. They need not apply to just the same things. The test of the theory is how it applies as a whole to the phenomena in question. Nevertheless Millikan deploys plentiful examples from the natural world, and appeals to our intuitions about them. But these intuitions are not definitive of the concepts in use. Rather, the theory is tested against the real-world examples, considered as empirical data. This approach frees Millikan from the traditional philosophical task of analysing ordinary language in order to spell-out the meanings of our concepts, a practice that is often stale and uninteresting. On the other hand, it does make LTOBC highly technical. The book unfolds as one long argument in nineteen chapters, each stage relying upon the concepts introduced in earlier chapters. It takes two whole chapters just to explain the concept of function that she employs. So many technical terms are eventually used that they have an index of their own. To make things easier I will avoid the technicalities. For our purposes, the benefits of summarizing outweigh the cost of some inaccuracy about the theory's subtleties.

Millikan's starting point is to think about functions in the evolutionary sense. As we saw in the last section, this involves looking at what a trait did in the historical past. Millikan came independently to the idea of characterising biological functions historically (aetiologically), although several philosophers had expressed this view in the 1970s. The idea is that some of the things a trait has done in the past will have contributed to the survival and reproduction of the organism carrying that trait. Consider moths' patterned wings as an example. A pattern that matches the background in a moth's environment will help that moth to survive until it can reproduce. The patterns on moth wings are inherited by offspring, so the moth's offspring will have the same pattern, which will in turn help them to survive and reproduce. Now consider a particular pattern on the wings of an individual forest-dwelling moth in the present day—a dappled motif, say. Part of the explanation of why that wing is dappled is that dappled wings in its ancestors helped them to survive and reproduce. The current pattern is caused by genes copied from moth to moth in the ancestral chain leading up to the present day. The ancestral dapples are part of a causal explanation of this copying process, and hence of why we see the individual's dappled wing today. That is the idea behind Millikan's biofunctions. In ancestors a trait did something (call it "X") that contributed to that trait being copied into the next generation, so that a causal explanation of why the trait exists now must advert in part to the trait doing X in the past—in that case X is one of the evolutionary functions of the trait. Applied to the moth case, camouflage is an evolutionary function of the dappled pattern on the moth's wing.

Next, think about what happened to all the moths in the past that had this camouflaged wing pattern (those that died as well as those that survived to reproduce). Some will have drifted into unsuitable environments or landed on backgrounds that did not match their wing pattern. In them, the wing pattern will not have aided survival. In others, for all the cunning of the pattern, a perceptive predator may have spotted them anyway, and gobbled them up. To function as camouflage, a wing pattern need not be effective all the time, or even most of the time. All that is needed is that camouflage sometimes helps a moth avoid getting caught, when without the camouflage it would have been. If there are some such occasions, then the wing pattern in one generation partly explains its being copied into the next generation. And if there are enough such occasions, then natural selection will explain why the moth population evolved so that they all eventually carry the camouflaged wing pattern (i.e., the ones that do not are selected against). Now focus on the occasions when the dappled wing pattern performed its evolutionary function in the past. Those occasions share a crucial characteristic: the moth must have been located against a dappled background. It is a truism that camouflage only works against the appropriate type of background. (Arctic hares stand out as nice white blobs in Cotswold Wildlife Park in England.) So it is a condition for the dappled wing pattern to perform its evolutionary function that the background be dappled, at least roughly. Only when the environment cooperates in this way can the evolutionary function be performed. Being on a dappled background is an environmental condition needed if the pattern (the trait) is to perform its evolutionary function. In general, there is some set of environmental conditions that are necessary to the performance of any given evolutionary function. These evolutionarily suitable conditions include lots of stable background material, like having sufficient nutrition, the surroundings not being too hot or cold, and so on. But they also include conditions peculiar to a particular trait, like being on a dappled background. All of these conditions, the general and the specific, are the evolutionary conditions for performance of that evolutionary function.

Those are the two key biological ideas behind Millikan's theory. The other parts of her theory are more specifically concerned with intentionality, although they rely on examples in the natural world too. To recap, the two ideas are: (1) that organisms and their parts have evolutionary functions, fixed by what those mechanisms did in their direct ancestors in the historical past; and (2) there are evolutionary conditions needed for the successful performance of those evolutionary functions. As a signpost to her writings, note that Millikan refers to (1) as "proper" functions and (2) as "normal" conditions ("Normal" in LTOBC). However, those terms have proved misleading. Commentators often forget that Millikan gives the terms technical meanings that do not fit their normal interpretation. The label "proper" makes it seem as if Millikan's theory starts with an assumption that traits have functions that it is proper for them to perform—that they are supposed to perform—whereas Millikan's theory actually explains rather than assumes the existence of natural purposes. The term "normal" is even more problematic, causing critics to forget that evolutionary functions may not be performed very often and that evolutionary conditions may be far from statistically normal—a fact emphasised by Millikan. Indeed, in some cases the evolutionary conditions for performance of an evolutionary function arise only very rarely (like the traits of plants in the Atacama desert designed only for when it rains, which it does on average once every hundred years).

Recall from the last chapter that the first move towards using evolutionary functions to account for intentionality is to divide representational systems into a producer system, a consumer system, and intermediate representations. For this to be a legitimate theoretical step there must be some principled way of making those distinctions without relying on the concepts of intentionality or representation. That is, the theory must be able to individuate the vehicles of representational content—the representations—before it goes on to tell a story about the content of those representations. Millikan's non-semantic means of individuating the vehicles of content proceeds as follows. First, find a mechanism that receives a variety of inputs and that does different things on different occasions, depending upon the input. That mechanism is then a candidate to be a consumer mechanism, and the variable items are candidate representations. Now look at the evolutionary function of this putative consumer mechanism, and consider the evolutionary conditions for its operation. In particular, see if the evolutionary conditions for its operation vary depending upon which variable item it consumes. The idea is that to be a consumer the system must do different things depending upon which representation it consumes, and that those different activities must each have an evolutionary function, each with different evolutionary conditions for its successful performance. In such cases there is a sense in which the consumer system is *assuming* that the world is a particular way—a different way in respect of each representation—in that it performs an activity which requires for its success that the world be that way. In such cases the consumer system makes different assumptions in response to different variable items. Therefore, we can say that the consumer system is *reading* the variable items as telling it how the world is and acting accordingly. Think of a table with the variable items in one column, the response of the consumer system in a second column, and a third column listing the evolutionary conditions specific to that response. Here is a portion of that table for the bee dance:

(1) Variable Items: Dances	(2) Response of the Consumer: Flight	(3) Specific Condition: *that there is nectar ...*
2 waggles at 45° from vertical	60 seconds flight at 45° to the direction of the sun	200 ft. away to the south west
3 waggles at 90° from vertical	90 seconds flight at 90° to the direction of the sun	300 ft. away to the west
5 waggles in vertical direction	150 seconds flight in the direction of the sun	500 ft. away to the south
...	...	...

Fig. 3 "Look-up table" for the bee dance (in part)

Columns (1) and (3) of the table list the way that the variable items must correspond to the world if the consumer system's activity is to be successful. For bee dances, the correspondence displays a mathematical function relating waggles to distances and angles to

The Theory

directions. However, the correspondence may be much more simple. Consider the table for the simpler example of the beaver splash:

(1) Variable Item	(2) Response of the Consumer	(3) Specific Evolutionary Condition
tail splash	diving under water	that there is danger nearby now

Fig. 4 Look-up table for the beaver splash

That is the whole of the table. The "variable" items only display minimal variation: splash or no splash. And there is only a very simple correspondence assumed by the functioning of the consumer mechanism. However, for all representational systems there is a way of listing the specific evolutionary condition for each variable item. That will be a list of what specific evolutionary condition is needed for the successful performance of the activity the consumer mechanism performs in relation to each variable item. Put another way, it is a list of the different assumptions the consumer system makes about the world when it is triggered by the different variable items. If we use the metaphor of the representation telling the consumer system that the world is a certain way, then the table is a list of what each different representation tells the consumer is the case.

Actually, the idea of a list is a simplification. No finite list could capture the relation between bee dances and what they represent since there is an infinite range of possible dances corresponding, for example, to all the possible directions between south and west. What allows consumer systems to respond appropriately to this entire range of representations is that there is a systematic relation between the dance and the direction represented: a mathematical transformation converts one into the other. Millikan stipulates that representational systems always display a systematic relationship between what is represented and variable features of the representation, so that the content can be derived by some appropriate mathematical transformation of the variable features of the representation.

Let's recap. How are the different systems—producer, consumer, and system of representations—individuated non-semantically? The answer runs as follows. Look for a mechanism triggered to perform a range of activities by a range of variable items, and if there is a transformation (like the look-up tables above) giving for each variable item a different evolutionary condition for the successful performance of that mechanism's activity, then the mechanism is a consumer system and the variable items are representations. In turn, the mechanism that produces the representations is a producer system. This is to state the theory in terms of a different function of the consumer system in response to each representation, with a different condition for each function. However, we can be more succinct and generalize across all the different outputs of the consumer system, and across their different conditions for successful performance of their functions. There is a condition which covers them all: that the representations should correspond to conditions in the world in the way given by the transformation. That is the evolutionary condition for the successful performance of the evolutionary function of the consumer mechanism.

Although Millikan's theory is forward-looking, relying on the consumer mechanism to fix content, she has similar things to say about the producer mechanism. The evolutionary conditions for the performance of the evolutionary function of the producer mechanism—what was the case when the mechanism did something that actually helped the survival of its ancestors—will include the fact that the representations corresponded to the world according to the entries in the look-up table. Ancestral beaver splashes contributed to survival only when there was danger. So agreeing with the look-up table is not the *function* of the producer system, but it is an evolutionary *condition* for the performance of its evolutionary function. For both producer and consumer systems, it is important to switch from focusing on functions to conditions for successful performance of evolutionary functions.

Now that the theory has a way of individuating representations non-semantically, it still has to say what each individual representation is about. That is, we still need to know how the content of each representation is determined—how to "pin the content on the representation." For Millikan's theory, that's easy—use the look-up tables! The content of a given representation is what the consumer system assumes it to mean. More precisely, a given representation is *about* the specific environmental conditions that were evolutionarily present when the consumer mechanism performed the evolved function of the activity triggered by that particular representation (i.e., the condition specific to the activity triggered by that representation).

Those are the bare bones of the theory. We saw in the last chapter that there was a worry whether teleosemantics could deliver contents with the required determinacy. The answer is that it does. Rival theories of intentionality based in causal covariance or information have a big

The Theory

problem with determinacy (discussed in chapter 1). A whole collection of difficulties in this area are referred to in the literature as "the disjunction problem." Millikan's theory was formulated with the disjunction problem in mind and so deals with the difficulties as it goes along. The problem is addressed by parts of the theory we have seen already: the forward-looking switch to the function of *consumers* rather than the circumstances in which representations are produced, the reliance on *explanations* of the evolutionary functions of those consumers, the focus on evolutionary *conditions* for the successful performance of those function, and the reference to those conditions *specific* to a given representation in the context of a range of representations consumed by the same mechanism. It is worth briefly spelling out how these aspects of the theory address the disjunction problems and deliver contents with the required determinacy.

A classic version of the disjunction problem applies to the fly's visual system discussed in the last chapter. Why is the frog not representing *fly* or *little black pellet*, since that is what it responds to? Causal theories consider the whole list of items which actually or potentially trigger a given representation, and so tend to ascribe contents that are a long disjunction of items on the list (hence the "disjunction" problem). Teleosemantics rules out these kinds of disjunctions because not all actual or potential triggers count, but only those things the presence of which are part of the evolutionary conditions for the successful performance of the evolutionary function of the mechanism. That rules out *little black pellet* as part of the content, since ingesting those has not contributed to the survival and reproduction of the mechanism.

Another way of posing this problem is to suggest that the frog's neural firing refers not to *flies* at all, but only to *little black things*. After all, the representation is triggered whenever the frog sees a little black thing passing across its visual field. Even if those little black things are lead pellets, the frog will go on darting its tongue at them. So, is the representation about *flies (flying prey)* or *little black things ("LBTs")*? Opponents of teleosemantics allege that Millikan's theory cannot adjudicate this dispute, and so cannot deliver the required determinacy. The argument is that the following is a good functional explanation of the operation of the system: the frog's optical system detects LBTs, which is beneficial because in the evolutionary environment LBTs correlate with flies. In fact, Millikan's theory has a decisive answer: when it comes to intentionality we should look at the evolutionary conditions for performance of the function of the consumer system.

LBTs are not part of the condition for successful performance. Evolution cares about flies, not LBTs. When the consumer (tongue dart) system functioned successfully, it caught a fly (more precisely, a nutritional flying object). That is a condition of its evolutionary functioning. So the tongue dart system is reading the neural firing as representing flies. That is what the representation refers to.

So teleosemantics takes in its stride two basic versions of the disjunction problem: "fly or pellet" and "little black things." Both concern alternative descriptions of objects out in the world. Another version of the disjunction problem asks about items in the causal chain between the object and the perceiver. How is it that teleosemantics delivers contents referring to objects out in the world rather than referring to items in the perceptual chain, like shadows on the retina or light waves in the air? For clarity I will change the example. Field mice have a simple mechanism that causes them to run for cover whenever a small shadow passes nearby. Many shadows are caused benignly, e.g., by falling leaves. But enough shadows are caused by aerial predators to make it worthwhile for evolution to have designed this reflex. Objectors to the theory say that teleosemantics cannot distinguish between *aerial predator* and *shadow* as being the content of the representation which is triggered (the representation that mediates between the optical production system and the consumer system that causes avoidance behavior). The objection mistakenly assumes that the system functions to detect shadows, with the world cooperating to ensure that shadows correlate with predators often enough to be useful. However, again in this case Millikan's theory gives a determinate answer to the question. The theory tells us to look to an evolutionary explanation for the survival and reproduction of the field mouse's mechanism. When we focus only on those occasions when the mechanism functioned so as actually to cause its own reproduction into the next generation, a causal explanation of that function will advert to detecting a *predator*. Put another way, the evolutionary condition that connects with successful performance of its evolutionary function is not *shadow*, about which evolution does not care, but *predator*, about which it does.

In other words, the focus on explaining the actual success of the organism's behavior leads to evolutionary conditions which concern the kinds of things *in the world* which evolution cares about: predators, food, mates, etc. The alternative—to look to the actual discriminatory capacities of the systems—is always a temptation, but one which is avoided by Millikan's teleosemantics.

For completeness I will consider a final version of the disjunction problem. This asks teleosemantics to arbitrate between various things as potential contents that are all evolutionary goods for the system in question. To distinguish from the other disjunction problems I will switch examples again. Let's return to the bacterium of the last chapter, with its magnetosome pointing downwards, to magnetic north. I said that the orientation of the magnetosome represents *direction of oxygen-free water*. But why does it not represent something more general like *safety* or *survival environment*, or even the very general *something evolutionarily beneficial*. That last is, of course, a condition for the successful performance of the evolutionary function of every evolved mechanism—*ex hypothesi*. This potential indeterminacy is again removed by different aspect of the theory, namely that a consumer system processes a range of representations and produces different behaviors in respect of each. Not all conditions for the successful performance of the functions of these behaviors count as contents, but only those *specific* to a particular representation. So background conditions like *being at an appropriate temperature* are ruled out as potential contents. As are general conditions like *being evolutionarily beneficial*. Millikan develops this idea further: the specific condition is the one which goes with what she calls the "most proximal normal explanation" of the operation of the mechanism (recall that "normal" does not mean usual or statistically normal). There is not space here to go into the details, so what I have said is only a partial clarification. But two important points should be noted. First, the "proximal" is not an arbitrary addition to the theory to deal with problem cases, but instead arises from the intuitive idea that the candidates for content are the conditions specific to a particular representation, in the context of a range of representations used by the same consumer system. Second, Millikan's theory will leave some indeterminacy about the content of representations in these cases, and in other examples of primitive representational systems. That level of indeterminacy is a virtue since it is implausible that such basic systems have as tightly-focused contents as do many representations in humans.

For example, the representation in the frog's optical system has a relatively unfocused content, something like *moving dark nutritious object*. This is nothing like the kinds of exact, focused contents possessed by human propositional attitudes. However, it is a virtue of teleosemantics that it ascribes these kinds of unfocused contents to primitive intentional systems. Only in higher representational systems is there sufficient complexity to generate focused contents. Furthermore, using terms like *moving dark nutritious object* to ascribe content to representations in simple systems can be very misleading, since the fly's representation does not itself contain any of the structure that we use to describe it. The frog has no representations corresponding to the components: movement, dark coloring, nutrition, physical object. Rather, it has a single undifferentiated representation, which we do our best to describe using the much more focused articulated concepts of human language. But this too is a merit of the theory. Determinacy increases and disjunction decreases in considering more complex representational systems, and it is only with the constituent structure and general-purpose nature of human intentionality that the kinds of highly-focused contents we are used to are achieved.

3.2   The Launch of LTOBC

It was a brave plan to try to apply Darwinism to the problem of intentionality. Other theoretical approaches were stuck, so it was worth persevering with a new direction. We have seen that Millikan had to realize the need for two major shifts to make the theory plausible. First, to switch to a forward-looking theory that focuses on the functions of the systems that consume representations. Second, not to rely directly on evolutionary functions to determine content, but to look instead to the evolutionary conditions under which those functions were performed. It took dedicated, concentrated thought to see the need for these shifts and to realize that they were promising ways to go. Then Millikan had to get all the details right. She could not expect a skeptical academic community simply to take the best ideas from her theory and embrace them. Rather, a theory will be attacked for all of its problems, even if they are peripheral to the main point. A good theory can be undermined if it is presented without sufficient attention to detail. Millikan worked on the details and gathered all this material into LTOBC. Knowing that it would be treated as the canonical statement of her position, LTOBC became a weighty book. All of this hard work proceeded in relative isolation, as Millikan continued to look after her young family and to teach part-time at the university. I suspect what drove her was a combination of ambition, determination, and her confidence in the importance of the new approach. Finally, she had a manuscript, but she needed a publisher. And a good one, if her book was to have a chance of being circulated widely enough to make an impact.

So Millikan sent a preliminary paper to Prof. Dan Dennett at Tufts University in nearby Massachusetts. By the early 1980s Dennett had forcefully established his reputation, both as a philosopher of mind, and as a theorist open to a dialogue among philosophy and the other cognitive sciences. He had not then achieved the fame outside philosophy brought by his books *Consciousness Explained* (1991) and *Darwin's Dangerous Idea* (1995), but he would be an influential ally. His philosophical approach was similar to Millikan's own, looking to the natural world and conceiving of philosophy as continuous with science. His theory of intentionality shared something with teleosemantics, since he thought true representational systems must have evolved (or have been designed by evolved organisms)—he took intentionality to be a "stance" for understanding such systems. On the other hand, he was a busy, famous professor and Millikan's paper came unsolicited from an unknown adjunct lecturer. Nevertheless, Dennett read the preliminary paper, and then the entire manuscript of LTOBC. That he read Millikan's work is a tribute to Dennett's enormous generosity. That he devoted much attention to it reflects its merit. Millikan received her draft book back covered in dense red ink, a wealth of corrections, queries, observations, and suggestions for improvement. Dennett also found her a publisher, the prestigious MIT Press, and publicly endorsed LTOBC in a foreword. So Millikan had her patron.

At the end of 1982, while LTOBC was in press and Millikan's theory still entirely unknown, she attended a talk at the American Philosophical Association by a visiting speaker from Britain, Prof. David Papineau. Imagine her surprise when he argued that evolutionary functions could be used to explain intentionality. Papineau's theory was not worked out in as much detail as Millikan's, but he had arrived independently at most of the important insights, including employing an aetiological theory of function and focusing on representation consumers as fixing content. After the talk, Millikan told Papineau excitedly about her work in the same area, and they became friends, meeting often over the years to discuss the nuances of teleosemantics. Papineau's views were subsequently published in a paper in 1984, the same year as LTOBC, and in two books: *Reality and Representation* (1987) and a chapter of his excellent *Philosophical Naturalism* (1993), as well as later papers.

Nineteen eighty-four also saw the publication of an influential paper by Prof. Jerry Fodor called "Semantics Wisconsin Style," recommending a teleological approach to intentionality. Fodor had made his name working at MIT on the cusp of philosophy and the empirical study of the mind, extending broadly Chomskian ideas to fields other than linguistics. He is famous for arguing that humans think in a "language of thought," manipulating word-like thoughts in systematic ways using the same kind of mechanism as that employed in a digital computer. His view that the mind performs computations over representations was widely accepted, and the language of thought hypothesis taken very seriously. However, by the early 1980s it became clear that he had a major problem because he too had no theory of intentionality. To be plausible Fodor needed some account of how the mind's representations refer as they do; of how the symbols in the language of thought get their meaning. He looked to teleology for an answer, as a suggestion in "Semantics Wisconsin Style," and worked out in more detail in a draft paper called "Psychosemantics, Or Where Do Truth Conditions Come From?" which circulated widely in 1985–1986. However, Fodor got stuck thinking in terms of the conditions in which representations are produced (he looked to teleology to specify the "normalcy" conditions under which representation production would be veridical). Facing seemingly intractable difficulties he abandoned teleosemantics. Fodor now has his own account of intentionality, published in *A Theory of Content and Other Essays* (1990), and rejects teleosemantics with the vehemence of the converted. Despite his change of heart, however, Fodor's flirtation with the theory served to give it greater currency, leading many more people to read about it and make up their minds for themselves. Fodor has since generously allowed his unpublished paper to be reprinted as a record of an important stage in the development of thinking about teleosemantics (in W. Lycan (ed.) 1990, *Mind and Cognition: A Reader*). Clearly teleosemantics was an idea whose time had come, and Millikan would not have to stand alone in defending the theory to the philosophical and psychological communities.

Millikan later discovered that the idea of appealing to natural teleology had been anticipated in a paper by Denis Stamp. Again, there was none of the detail of LTOBC, but this was a further indication that people were ready to think along lines that formerly would have been heretical.

So LTOBC gained an international reputation and Millikan was recognized as one of the most important living philosophers of mind. Invitations followed and Millikan soon had a busy schedule of lectures, conferences, and seminars around the world. Her ideas have since developed in many new directions, but she remains in great demand for deep thinking and the ability to draw simultaneously from traditional philosophy and natural science. She has as many readers in psychology as in philosophy, and this is reflected in her speaking circuit. Eminence has come not only in the form of job offers from top universities, but also in being invited to deliver some prestigious lectures, like Oxford University's Gareth Evans Memorial Lecture, and the Jean Nicod series at the *Centre National des Recherches Scientifique* in Paris.

As well as important work in several other areas, some of which I will discuss in later chapters, Millikan has written more on teleosemantics. Although LTOBC remains the canonical statement of her theory, she published a summary in the influential *Journal of Philosophy* in 1989 ("Biosemantics") and a subsequent collection of papers called *White Queen Psychology and Other Essays for Alice* (1993). She describes *White Queen* as a retrospective introduction to the difficulties of LTOBC.

Taking stock, we have seen so far that teleosemantics provides a potential new way of naturalizing intentionality. The power is worthy of the excitement it generated. As yet we have only considered its application in relatively simple organisms, where the evolved functions of the representational system are relatively clear. In the next section, we will start to see how the theory deals with more complex systems.

3.3 Derived Functions

Bee dances, beaver splashes, frog reflexes, and bacteria are all a long way from human intentionality. In section 3.4 we will see how Millikan characterizes the distinctively human case. However, even in simpler systems something more needs to be said about the application of natural selection to intentionality. That is because it is possible for many organisms to produce entirely new representations, never seen in the history of that organism, representing something that neither they, nor their ancestors, have ever encountered before. How can these novel items have their content fixed by a theory that relies upon evolutionary functions?

Consider an example. Like us, chimpanzees can recognize one another by their faces. Suppose they have a dedicated face-recognition mechanism, the job of which is to store a perceptual memory of encountered faces in order to recognize individuals again and to differentiate them from other individuals. A young chimp may use this mechanism to store a perceptual exemplar of one of its cousins, Swinger, and it may well be that no chimp in the history of the species has ever looked quite like Swinger. Then this representation of Swinger will be entirely novel in the history of the species. There is no history of ancestry to rely upon to fix the function of the Swinger-detecting mechanism. Nevertheless, it is easy to see that the specific Swinger-detecting mechanism does have an evolutionary function, namely to recognize Swinger, the individual. In virtue of what is that its evolutionary function? The answer derives from the evolutionary function of the face-detection mechanism. That mechanism evolved to enable chimps to recognize other individuals by their faces. So although the representation of Swinger may be novel, it is produced in the normal way by a mechanism that does have a history and an evolutionary function—the evolutionary function of producing sub-mechanisms that recognize individuals by their faces. Although the particular sub-mechanism that recognizes Swinger may be entirely new, it derives a function from the evolutionary function of the learning mechanism that produced it. So the Swinger-recognizing sub-mechanism does indeed have the function of recognizing Swinger, the individual, by his face.

The example illustrates a powerful new idea: items without an evolutionary history of their own may nevertheless have a biological function, which derives from the evolutionary function of some mechanism selected in the past to produce sub-mechanisms of the same type. In Millikan's terminology the evolved mechanism has a *relational* function, and the new product of that mechanism a *derived* function. These terms apply even to simple, nonintentional mechanisms. Millikan uses the example of the chameleon's skin. The mechanism that makes a chameleon change color has a relational evolutionary function: to produce a skin color that matches the chameleon's background. It is by performing exactly that function in the past that the mechanism has contributed to reproduction of the species, and hence reproduction of the mechanism itself. But a particular shade of skin color adopted on a particular occasion may be entirely new in the history of the species, perhaps because an individual has strayed into a new environment. Nevertheless, this new shade has a function deriving from the function of the relational mechanism. Schematically:

Relational function:
  to match whatever the background looks like at the time
Particular background on a given occasion:
  red and green polka dots
Novel derived function of the skin color on that occasion:
  to match red and green polka dots

The Theory

Bee dances also display this structure. The evolutionary function of the consumer mechanism requires a dance with a direction that matches the location of the nectar visited by the representation producer (recall: the dance should match the location according to the look-up table that can be read off the conditions for performance of the evolutionary function of the consumer mechanism). That is a relational function. The derived function of a particular dance is to match the location of a particular source of nectar.

Relational and derived functions are essential to account for the capacity to represent something never before encountered in the history of the individual or of the species. Where we can ascribe to a device a quite specific relational evolutionary function, then that relational function will be informative about the function of the derived mechanisms. So with the chimps' face-recognition mechanism the relational function licenses the attribution of a quite specific content to the resultant representations: they each represent the face of some individual. Which individual is represented is determined by the operation of that relational mechanism in a particular case, that is, it depends upon the particular learning history. Where the relational function is more abstract it will have correlatively less to say about the content of a particular representation. More of the content determination must advert to the individual circumstances under which the new representation was learned. In such cases intentionality still derives ultimately from evolutionary functions, but the content of a particular representation is fixed much more by the circumstances of individual learning history than by the evolutionary history of the species. That is to say, the characteristics of intentionality—aboutness, misrepresentation, and normativity—are founded in derived functions, themselves deriving from relational evolutionary functions. But the content of particular representations is fixed more by individual history than by evolution.

When considering human intentionality this point becomes acutely relevant. It is plausible that humans have very general-purpose mechanisms for producing novel representations. For example, it is widely thought that humans have a general-purpose mechanism for producing new desires from existing desires by means of practical reasoning. That mechanism is, as yet, imperfectly understood, and there remain disputes as to what the evolutionary (relational) function of such a general purpose mechanism is. Some other means for forming new desires are better understood, like classical and instrumental conditioning. But even in those cases the relational function of the mechanism is hard to characterize in a way that tells us much about the contents of the representations it produces. Similarly, we have mechanisms for producing new concepts, which can form part of novel beliefs, some of which are domain-specific, and others more general. These new concepts will be used in producing beliefs that have their content fixed by the way they interact with desires to produce behavior—if the actions selected by a given belief in different circumstances all require for their success some particular state of affairs, then that state of affairs just is the content of the belief. However, the belief-forming mechanisms are not thereby irrelevant to the determination of content. In order to pin down the evolutionary functions of the various systems involved in producing human beliefs and desires, including those which operate in a general-purpose fashion, much more must be known about how these various systems actually work.

The poor understanding of these relational functions presents practical problems for the application of teleosemantics. It does not undermine teleosemantics' claim to naturalize intentionality. But it does leave us without a formula that we can apply to a particular concrete representation in order to ascertain what its content is. Compare Newton's theory of gravitation. It not only tells us in what the force of gravitation consists. It also allows us to calculate the actual force due to gravity between any two bodies of known mass and separation. Currently, teleosemantics only does the first part: it tells us in what representation consists. The theory makes the perfectly reasonable assumption that there are general principles of cognitive psychology yet to be discovered that explain how an infant develops various kinds of concepts and learns to employ them in a way that is adapted to the particular environment it lives in. That this part of the story is currently incomplete is no objection to teleosemantics. But it does make it harder to apply and test the theory by reference to examples, and hence to make a convincing case for its validity. We have seen in chapter 1 how definitional theories of meaning have been rejected mainly because of their inability to produce examples and the implausibility of the examples that are offered (see section 1.2(3)). Until there is a persuasive consensus as to what the relational evolutionary functions of the human belief/desire generating mechanisms are, teleosemantics can't even be tested in that way. So, despite the fact that teleosemantics has provided a naturalization of intentionality, a suspicion of incompleteness remains.

That suspicion should be dispelled when it is remembered that the job of a theory of intentionality is to say in what the aboutness, misrepresentation, and normativity of representation consists, not to tell us the content of individual representations. Furthermore, in practical terms we are not stuck, not knowing what the contents of our thoughts are. Fortunately, there is no need in practice to advert to evolutionary relational functions and the circumstances of individual learning to ascribe contents to people's beliefs and desires; we should continue to do so in the usual, practical, everyday fashion. But these everyday techniques of content ascription give us access to contents in fact determined by the poorly understood relational mechanisms, together with the individual circumstances which confer derived functions on all the new representations that an individual develops in her lifetime. Thus, to see the validity of teleosemantics, two features of the theory must be accepted. First, that everyday means of content ascription give us access to contents in fact determined by the abstract relational functions of mechanisms which, in humans, are as yet poorly understood. Second, that much of the determinacy of the content of the representations a human develops in her lifetime derives from the individual's particular circumstances—what she has encountered in her learning history—and not from that in virtue of which the representations are contentful in the first place, namely evolutionary function.

The powerful idea of relational and derived functions is both useful in understanding biological functions in general, and indispensable to account for learning. Learning produces new abilities the functions of which derive from the purposes of the learning mechanism. To the extent that learning occurs by a mechanism of generating alternatives and selecting those that meet some criterion, it too could be characterised as a Darwinian process. And if that were right, there would be no need for the machinery of relational and derived proper functions, since the learned items would have their functions directly as a result of this selectional process. However, it is unlikely that much learning is like this. Even in cases where a range of possibilities are generated to be selected amongst, there appears to be some preselection of alternatives, constrained by the purpose of the learning mechanism. And, since there are learning mechanisms like imprinting and imitating that operate directly, without generating and selecting amongst a range of competing items, the theory of relational and derived functions will be indispensable to account for the functions of things learned in these ways.

The Theory

Recall the discussion at the end of the last section about the disjunction problem. We saw there that teleosemantics delivers as the content of representations the sort of things in the world that evolution cares about ("target" features like prey, predators, mates) rather than the things actually discriminated by perceptual systems ("perceptual" features like smells, sounds, patterns of light, etc.). The presence of learning mechanisms adds an important elaboration onto that basic account, because it allows for systems whose function is first to produce representations which covary with perceptual features, so that these may later be used for many diverse purposes. To see this, notice that the output of a perceptual mechanism may have no direct connection to behavior. Think of the rat's olfactory system, and suppose that before a rat has done any learning the system causes no overt behavior. All it does is to produce items that in fact covary with some range of smells. Considering the olfactory system causally, suppose one of these items (call it R) is caused by a particular pheromone and nothing else, and another (call it F) only by complex carbohydrates. Supposing that the rat can already recognize some useful categories, like food and conspecifics, it can then learn to associate the internal items R and F with those target features. When it learns that R is a sign of rats the learning system produces a new sub-mechanism $S\text{-}M_1$ that causes cautious-approach behavior whenever R is produced. Similarly, F comes to be associated with food, producing a new sub-mechanism $S\text{-}M_2$ that causes salivation whenever F is produced. The relational function of the associative learning mechanism is something like this: when a perceptual item reliably co-occurs with some target feature, carry out in relation to the perceptual item the behavior relevant to the target feature. The derived functions of the new sub-mechanisms are thus:

$S\text{-}M_1$: to behave in response to R in a way appropriate to other rats
$S\text{-}M_2$: to behave in response to F in a way appropriate to food

The evolutionary function of the olfactory mechanism is to produce devices that are available for this sort of associative learning. It is not a condition for the performance of the evolutionary function of the perceptual mechanism that its deliverances covary with any one specific target feature, like food or conspecifics. Rather, the only condition that will explain the varied purposes to which the perceptual mechanism is put in learning, in the organism's history, is that the devices it produces should coincide with certain smells—that it

The Theory

produces device R when a particular pheromone is present and device F when complex carbohydrates are present. In our example, the rat learned to use these smells as signs of other rats and food respectively. But because these associations were learned and not prefixed, the rat could learn to use these perceptual devices as signs of other things. (Assume for the purpose of the example that a variety of different smell-behavior associations have been useful in the rat's evolutionary past.)

As a result of learning, an organism uses a range of perceptual outputs for a variety of different behavioral purposes. In general, these different behaviors will have diverse conditions for their successful performance. But the requirement that the perceptual representation should coincide with the perceptual feature is a shared condition. Millikan talks of this as *triangulating* across the different uses for which a perceptual representation is used. In organisms with learning mechanisms, the deliverances of the perceptual system are employed for a diverse range of functions. Therefore, the content of the representations they produce triangulates on perceptual features like smells, colors, and sounds, rather than target features like prey, predators, and conspecifics. Some commentators have argued that teleosemantics cannot account for the ability to represent perceptual features. The answer is that—in organisms that learn—teleosemantics can give an account (via the usual idea of conditions that explain the successful past performance of evolutionary functions) of the existence of representations with perceptual features as contents, as well as representations referring to target features.

To recap, there is a wide gulf between the intentionality found in simple organisms and the content of human thoughts. However, we have seen several theoretical resources that move towards bridging the gap: the idea of relational and derived functions, the role of learning, the representation of perceptual features, and the idea of triangulation across diverse functions. In the next section we will see what more is needed to arrive at distinctively human intentionality.

3.4 Higher Level Intentionality

In Millikan's view, none of the theory above is supposed to account for distinctively human representational content. She makes a persuasive case that teleosemantics provides a naturalization of intentionality across a whole range of intentional systems. But she also accepts that something distinctive is going on in the human case.

Millikan therefore goes on to say something about distinctively human cognition, although it need not be part of the task of naturalizing intentionality to say what is special about the human case. To preview, the distinctive features of human thought identified by Millikan are broadly similar to what is distinctive about human language. But first comes a step towards complexity that we share with some other animals.

Even primitive intentionality involves relational and derived functions. In the last section we saw that more sophisticated organisms that can learn from experience can form more complex representational systems, with derived functions that inherit more of their content from the circumstances of individual learning than from the evolutionary relational function from which they derive. Furthermore, some such learning systems can represent perceptual features, in addition to target features. This more complex apparatus is found in many organisms. There was no claim that it is distinctively human. The next step towards the human case is also found in other animals. It introduces a further level of representational complexity, but one which is again not distinctively human (or at least, may not be—theorists disagree).

Many human thoughts are part of an integrated system of beliefs and desires. Beliefs represent what is the case and desires represent what the agent would like to be the case. These two propositional attitudes can contain the same contents, but have different directions of fit. Take the content that *I have a son*. A belief with this content should match what is the case in the world—beliefs about my family should be adjusted to fit the facts. That is, beliefs have *indicative* contents. On the other hand, the desire that I have a son is much more interesting, motivating me to act in ways that lead to its fulfilment. So, in a sense, desires "require" the world to change so that the world fits the desire. Thus, desires act as motivators; they have *imperative* contents. For this reason, the belief/desire system contains a new kind of representational sophistication, namely the differentiation of representations into at least two types, imperative and indicative, with different directions of fit to the world.

The representations in simple systems do not display this distinction. The magnetosome in a magnetotactic bacterium both represents the direction of oxygen-free water and tells the bacterium to swim in that direction. That is because it is a normal condition for the successful performance of its evolutionary function both that there be oxygen-free water in the direction indicated and that the bacterium swim in the direction indicated. So it has both indicative content, like a belief, and imperative content, like a desire. In Millikan's view simple representational systems always have this undifferentiated character. They are both indicative and imperative at once, what she calls "pushmi-pullyu" (push-me, pull-you) representations. Bee dances, beaver splashes, and the frog's fly-triggered neural response are all pushmi-pullyu representations. To ascribe a purely indicative content, we must find an internal state that is supposed to co-vary with the world, and is used for a variety of purposes to initiate different actions. So the differentiation into indicative and imperative representations is a relatively sophisticated feature of cognition. Which is not to say that it is distinctive of human cognition. Nor does Millikan deny that humans have pushmi-pullyu representations. Indeed, they may be found in some of our more basic systems, like the immune system. Our conscious intentions (what we intend to do—not to be confused with the intentionality of representations) are probably also pushmi-pullyu representations. Once we have formed the intention to go to the doctor, say, this representation may act both as a motivator, telling us what to do, and as an indicator, telling us what we will in fact do, so that we can plan other things around it (e.g., I intend to go to the doctor on Tuesday afternoon so I won't schedule a meeting for that time).

So the differentiation of pushmi-pullyu representations into indicative and imperative representations is another step towards the complexity of human cognition. A further characteristic of the human belief/desire system is its general-purpose nature. We are able to reason from a set of desires, via beliefs, to sub-goals which are further desires, and we do this in a relatively general-purpose way. We can also reason from a stock of beliefs to further beliefs. These are extremely powerful tools. It seems that, in principle, any fact and any goal can be represented, and in carrying out a piece of reasoning, any of our other beliefs and desires may be brought into play, if relevant. If the system is indeed general in its application and operation, then that is a remarkable achievement. How does the system operate in such a general-purpose way? That is not well understood. It must function so that the ways in which representations are processed and translated into action fit together with the ways in which those representations are produced in response to the environment. Theorists do not have a very good idea how that is achieved. Attempts to model such general-purpose reasoning by computer programs come up against the difficulty of assessing in real time what pieces of information are potentially relevant for the purpose of making a particular inference. Maybe the general-purpose nature of our belief/desire system is something that is distinctively human. On the other hand, we may be wrong in thinking that the human system is truly a general-purpose reasoner.

Millikan's account of what is distinctive about human intentionality has close ties to the general-purpose nature of our representation and reasoning. The differentiation into indicative and imperative representations is a step towards human contents, but she makes two further observations about what more is distinctively human, both of which concern the structure of human thoughts and what we can do with that structure.

Millikan's claims arise from the observation that the structure of at least some human thought is language-like, and that this is distinctively human. The features of natural language which carry over into distinctively human thought are: its generality and its subject-predicate structure, bringing with it the possibility of negation. These features of language can be illustrated briefly. Generality arises from the ability to re-use the components of a sentence in other contexts. For example, the word "John" from the sentence "John is tall" can be re-used with the predicate "is young" to give the new sentence "John is young." Generality arises from the fact that sentence components (words and phrases) can be recombined in arbitrary ways, carrying their meanings with them. (The constraints on how words can be combined to form sentences arise from their grammatical types, not from their meanings.) Subject-predicate structure is the way many simple sentences divide into two different components. One component, the subject, picks out some object (e.g., John) and the other component predicates some property of that object (e.g., is tall). It is essential to the nature of predicates that they admit of negation (e.g., is not tall), so that they are opposed to one another and have contraries. By contrast, subject terms do not admit of negation: there is no such thing as "Not-John," which refers to an object. We read "Not John is young" as "John is not young," negating the predicate, not the subject term.

Applying these linguistic features to human thoughts, Millikan's first claim is that humans are distinctive in having thoughts containing predicates, which admit of negation and exclude their contraries. The representations in simpler systems, like bee dances and magnetosomes, do not have this subject-predicate structure. Millikan's second main claim about the structure of distinctively human thought connects with her work on concepts, to be discussed in chapter 4. Her observation concerns the generality with which we can re-use the constituents of thought. Human thoughts that have the subject-predicate structure (or more complex structures still) contain parts. For example, the belief that *dogs bark* contains the concepts DOG and BARKING. Gottlob Frege, a highly-influential nineteenth-century German philosopher and the founder of modern logic, observed that these parts derive their meaning from the roles they play in whole thoughts. Nevertheless the component concepts can be re-used in other contexts to state different things. So DOG can be reused in the thought that dogs are mammals and BARKING can be reused in the thought that seals bark. Millikan makes a persuasive case that some human cognition displays this kind of generality—empirical concept possessed by a thinker can be combined with any other. Thus, if you can think *dogs bark* and can also think *seals are mammals* you will have all four of those concepts, so you will be able to think *dogs are mammals* and *seals bark*. Of course, there are constraints on the generality requirement. For example, the terms must be combined in structurally the right sort of way, e.g., subject terms cannot be paired directly with other subject terms (JOHN MARY is badly formed as a potential thought). But within these structural constraints any empirical concept can be recombined with any other to produce a truth-evaluable content.

To recap, the differentiation of pushmi-pullyu representations into indicative and imperative representations is a step towards the complexity of human cognition. However, in Millikan's view, two further-related features characterize the distinctively human case. First, our thoughts have a subject-predicate structure with the associated possibility of negation. Second, a generality constraint applies to the constituents of many of our thoughts: they can be recombined in arbitrary ways to produce new truth-evaluable contents, the constituents making the same contribution to truth conditions in each case.

3.5 Objections and Responses

In this final section of the chapter, I will consider three lines of objection to Millikan's teleosemantics. The first arises from general worries about the Darwinian theory of natural selection. The second is an important philosophical objection concerning inaccessible contents. And the third objects that teleosemantics makes content contingent on facts about evolutionary history.

(1) Reliance on Darwinism

Darwinism has mixed academic credentials. It is one of the most important theories in the sciences and offers an explanation of some of the most puzzling aspects of the natural world, like the origin of complexity and apparent design. On the other hand, notoriously, many claims about the evolutionary functions of psychological traits are implausible and unsupported. The academic disciplines of sociobiology, human behavioral ecology, and evolutionary psychology make an industry of offering evolutionary explanations of a whole range of cognitive functions. However, work in these areas is often very badly executed, especially in versions produced for popular consumption. Some of the academic output is more tailored to grabbing popular attention than to achieving theoretical rigour. Theories often rely upon unevidenced claims about the environment in which traits evolved, typically unsupported assertions about the Pleistocene era reinforced only by the prejudices of "common sense." Indeed, sometimes a trait is argued to be very likely to be found in humans because of the way things supposedly were in the Pleistocene (e.g., men were the macho hunters, whereas women went around meekly gathering fruit), and then the "existence" of the trait is offered as evidence that conditions in the Pleistocene really were that way. When the only basis for thinking the trait exists is an argument from the nature of Pleistocene society, this scheme or reasoning is viciously circular. Work in this area is hampered by the difficulty of getting at the necessary evidence. Little is known about the behavioral and social conditions in which humans evolved today's cognitive traits, because brains decay and behavior leaves few traces in the fossil record. Empirical work marshals evidence from diverse sources in an attempt to overcome these problems: comparing the psychological traits of related extant species, like humans and chimpanzees; analyzing DNA of different species to produce phylogenetic trees, and where possible, phylogenies of traits from their genes; subjecting human and prehuman fossils to meticulous study; and so on. The key difference between psychological traits and other biological functions is that it is very hard to discern the functional organization of the brain. Scientists were able to work out how the circulatory system works by looking at the physical parts (heart, arteries, veins, etc.) and working out what they do. As yet we have only the crudest idea of the functional parts of human cognition. Yet these are the components to which evolutionary functions should be ascribed. To overcome this obstacle, hypotheses about evolutionary function are themselves used as means of individuating components. That is one of the means that can be employed to try to address these nearly intractable questions, but the whole enterprise remains, at the moment, radically under-constrained.

The Theory

Critics sometimes deploy these worries about the evolutionary psychology of human cognitive traits to attack teleosemantics' use of evolutionary functions to naturalize intentionality. That criticism is misplaced, since teleosemantics does not rely upon ascribing particular functions to particular psychological systems. Rather, it makes a much more general claim about what intentionality consists in. Strictly, it is not a task for the theory of intentionality to say what are the evolved functions of different kinds of representational systems. All that teleosemantics need say is that all intentional systems contain representations that are intentional in virtue of their mediating role between producer and consumer systems, and that the content of the representations is given by the evolutionary conditions for the performance of the evolutionary function of the consumer system. In short, teleosemantics relies only upon very general features of Darwinism. It adopts the relatively uncontentious claim that biological functions should be explained by Darwinian evolution. Teleosemantics need have nothing to do with the more implausible just-so stories of evolutionary psychology.

The same objection and response has been made to Darwinism in traditional biology. In ascribing to the human heart the function *to pump blood,* biologists do not look at examples of past organs that did and did not pump blood effectively. Ancestors' hearts are not available to study. But biologists do not need to examine the fossil record nor to make an analysis of the ecological conditions in which hearts arose. Rather, they look at human anatomy and ascribe functions to parts on the basis of what those parts actually do in healthy individuals. This seems at first to have nothing to do with the historical approach to function. But, as we saw at the start of this chapter, without an aetiological theory of function there was a problem as to how what a trait does now (pumps blood) could be explained by the effect that that action would have (circulating blood). So the aetiological theory was needed to say how functional ascription could be explanatory. It is also required to underpin the normativity of those functions. It is widely (but not universally) agreed that what makes it the case that a leaky heart valve is malfunctioning is the fact that it is not working in the way ancestors' heart valves did when hearts contributed to the survival of the species and reproduction of the trait. So evolutionary considerations underpin the distinction between function and malfunction—the normativity of function attributions—but the best practical way to discover what those functions are remains the traditional one: to see how things actually work. The only difference with cognitive traits is that it is much more difficult to work out how, in the here and now, things actually work.

This line of response to the objection must be qualified. We have seen that other theories of intentionality are assessed both from general theoretical considerations, and on the basis of examples of what the theory says about specific representations. Teleosemantics has lots of such examples of intentionality in special-purpose systems, like bee dances and beaver splashes, where it seems to deliver the right results. But it can say less about intentionality in human cognitive systems, because much less is known about the components of these systems and how they function. In a way teleosemantics has written an uncashed check. Only when the work of understanding human cognition is nearly complete can teleosemantics be appraised for what it says about actual human cognition. It is an extremely promising account of what intentionality consists in. But critics will not be convinced until it can be demonstrated that teleosemantics really does apply to the functions of the systems that combine in human cognition. Of course, this worry—does the theory fit with the empirical details?—applies to almost every other extant philosophical theory of content.

The point can be illustrated by looking briefly at some recent work in experimental psychology, concerning concepts and categorization. This empirical work attempts to discover how people are able to divide the world up into different categories. One fruitful line of enquiry explores our use of stored prototypes: typical but nondefinitive features of items in the category. From Millikan's point of view this research concerns implementational mechanisms. These psychological theories of concepts and content are not in conflict with her philosophical theory of what content consists in. However, this empirical work could eventually help teleosemantics by elucidating the nature of the relational evolutionary functions that underpin human general-purpose cognition. So rather than conflicting, this work is part of the picture which must be filled in if teleosemantics is to be fully confirmed in its application to human cognition.

Culture makes the reliance on evolutionary functions even more complicated. Many human cognitive traits have evolved, not in response to external environmental features, but because of the ecological environment created by conspecifics and their cognitive traits. Such "cultural" mechanisms arguably provide a nongenetic locus for functional evolution. In the recent history of humans, there has probably been a complex interaction between gene-based evolution and the purely cultural evolution of cognitive traits. None of these considerations need undermine the claim that intentionality derives ultimately from evolutionary functions. It just means that that claim must be defended in a more subtle way in the human case to deal with the nuances of human evolution.

As an example, consider again the function of logical negation discussed in the previous section. Millikan's view is that negation (along with logical conjunction and disjunction, and many other concepts) derives its identity from the special functions it performs, and that those functions are distinctive of human cognition. But what kinds of functions are they? Did they arise solely by gene-based evolution, or are they the result of co-evolution between humans' genetic and cultural resources? It is not even clear that these questions are well-formed as they stand. The whole complex of genes and developmental environment is probably better seen as constituting a wider developmental system that gives rise to mature traits that are stable over the generations. In my view, teleosemantics will become more plausible as an account of the nature of intentionality as the actual functioning of features of human cognition like these logical operations comes to be better understood.

In summary, there are legitimate concerns about our ability to give evolutionary explanations of cognitive traits, but these concerns do not undermine teleosemantics since its claims are made at a much more abstract level—not about the functions of particular human traits, but about the nature of intentionality in general, human or otherwise. However, teleosemantics (like most theories of intentionality) will not be fully confirmed until it can be assessed in the light of more detailed empirical evidence about the nature of human cognition, and tested against examples. Such test cases require a better understanding than we currently have of the articulation of human cognition into its component functions. Although that articulation may itself rely upon evolutionary considerations as one (weak) source of evidence, it also throws up complexities because of the role of culture in the evolution of human cognitive traits. Furthermore, in the human case, teleosemantics holds that the content of many particular individual representations is fixed mostly by the circumstances of individual learning history, and relatively little by the highly abstract relational functions of the mechanisms by which new representations are developed. That fact makes the role of Darwinism in the theory seem even less important. None of this undermines teleosemantics. Indeed, the teleosemantic approach can aid empirical research by allowing experimental hypotheses to be framed in the light of a better understanding of the nature of cognition. But even if teleosemantics is correct, there is still a lot to do before we properly understand human cognition.

(2) Inaccessible Contents

Next we consider an important philosophical objection to the theory. It is a technical misgiving, concerning philosophical issues of realism and antirealism. If you don't already have a philosophical interest in these issues, you won't lose anything by skipping this section.

This objection to teleosemantics concerns our ability to represent what are called "inaccessible contents." A caricatured version of the worry goes as follows: Natural selection can only care about what is causally relevant to survival and reproduction. But distant areas of the universe have never been causally relevant to the survival and reproduction of any organism on Earth. So how can humans have representations with contents like *Sirius is 10^{14} kilometres from the Earth* (which we do)?

The simple reply relies on the generality of human cognition. We take concepts that achieve their content in one context, where they are causally relevant, and reuse them in other contexts where they are not. So the concepts of METER and TEN TIMES are causally relevant in all sorts of everyday contexts. But the application of them together enough times can create inaccessible contents (*ten times ten times ... meters*). Those inaccessible contents can be referred to in virtue of the re-using terms which get their content from everyday contexts.

The debate then becomes much more subtle. The nuanced view of the objection is that the right content in the first place for the everyday use of METER is *100 cm and not causally inaccessible.* The idea is that the underlined sub-clause is always there, but it is irrelevant when the concept is used in everyday contexts. The objector argues that it is a consequence of relying on natural selection that these kinds of sub-clauses will constrain the content of all representations whenever they are used, so that when they are combined into complexes like TEN TIMES TEN TIMES ... METERS, the content is *ten times ten times ... meters and not causally inaccessible.* To sketch an answer, there are three strands to teleology's response: (1) human general-purpose cognition re-uses representational resources in a range of contexts, as mentioned above; (2) the conditions for successful performance of a *derived* function can fall outside anything in evolutionary history, provided they lie within the range of the kind of conditions that explain the performance of the evolutionary function of the relational mechanism from which they derive; and (3) the properties employed in scientific enquiry have some scale of naturalness, so that a gerrymandered property like *meter and not causally inaccessible* is less suitable to appear in an empirical theory than the commonsense *meter*. As I have argued above, greater determinacy comes with greater representational complexity. The details of Millikan's theory as set out in LTOBC show how the appropriate amounts of determinacy are achieved at the appropriate levels of representational complexity. It takes the complexity of the human representational system to represent inaccessible contents. But the challenge was only to explain how humans can represent inaccessible contents; simpler organisms probably cannot. As you would expect, the details of the debate about inaccessible contents become very intricate, and there is not scope to give a definitive answer here. It is enough to observe that the objection is surmountable.

(3) The historical nature of evolutionary functions

The final type of objection we will consider arises from the historical nature of evolutionary functions. The project is to explain intentionality, but remember that the usefulness of intentionality in the first place is that ascribing representational content is a way of predicting and explaining organisms' behavior. Why should historical functions be any good for that? Surely we should be more interested in how things currently operate.

This is a deep and important conceptual problem that teleosemantic theorists must grapple with. Millikan has some persuasive answers, but the debate is far from closed. A first observation is that evolutionary functions are a good guide to current organization, since current circumstances are much like those in the evolutionary past. But that invites the question why current functions, tailored to current circumstances, are not an even better guide. Millikan's answer appeals to the generality of the explanations she offers. She is attempting to explain biological functions in species. These are historical categories and range over classes of things which, though lacking any defining physical similarity in the here and now, share properties in virtue of their history. For example, bird wings and bat wings are very different, but they share one of their biological functions because they evolved to solve the same ecological problem. A grain of analysis that looked only at current organization would, according to Millikan, miss out on the generalization under which bird wings and bat wings perform the same function. Even if the example is questioned on the basis that there are current functional similarities between bird wings and bat wings, the point remains plausible: that ascription by current function may miss some of the generalizations that are available when taking the perspective of historical function.

Millikan can also argue that, even where there are current categories that divide the world in the same way as the historical ones, the historical functions have conceptual priority for the reasons which motivate her theory—they are the source of the normativity of attributions of function and intentionality, and only aetiological functions can be explanatory, as well as predictive. Yet again, the debate becomes much more difficult when considering human contents. In our case, much of the content determination for particular representations derives from the circumstances of individual learning and development, prompting the worry that intentionality really derives from these individual circumstances and not from evolutionary functions. However, if these are individual circumstances of learning, they are still historical conditions, rather than current ones.

Vigorous debate continues about these three types of objection to teleosemantics, and others. It is not yet clear in whose favor the disputes will be resolved. Several things are, however, evident. First, Millikan's theory has quickly risen to prominence as one of the most promising ways of naturalizing intentionality. Second, it has served to reinvigorate a field of inquiry that had reached a conceptual impasse. Third, the details of LTOBC provide plausible answers to many of the objections commonly raised against teleosemantics. Fourth, teleosemantics could be improved in its plausibility were more known about the structure and functions of the components of human psychology, which remains an extremely open area of investigation. And finally, that this feeling of incompleteness in the application of Millikan's theory to human cognition need not undermine her claim that the ultimate source of the aboutness, normativity, and capacity for misrepresentation in all intentional systems, including ours, is to be found in evolutionary functions.

4
Concepts

4.1 Introduction: What Are Concepts?

So far we have been considering the nature of intentionality in general. We have seen that Millikan's teleosemantics is a powerful proposal for naturalizing intentionality, and hence for explaining how there can be a place in the natural world for aboutness, misrepresentation, and its associated normativity. We saw that teleosemantics was most easily applied to special purpose systems and intentionality in lower organisms. It also provides a foundation for naturalizing human intentionality, although there is much more work to do to provide a satisfying explanation of the contents of human thoughts. The last chapter looked at how the representations in more complex intentional systems can have constituent structure. Although this is not unique to human intentionality, a satisfying account of how these constituents operate will provide a deeper understanding of human cognition. Millikan has done much to fill in this picture with her work on concepts, appearing in various published papers and culminating in *On Clear and Confused Ideas: An Essay About Substance Concepts* (2000). That work is the subject of this chapter.

"Concept" is used by theorists in lots of different ways, and it is easy to get in a muddle. You might think that to produce a theory of

Concepts

concepts you must first elucidate the CONCEPT concept. And to do *that*, you need a theory of concepts. And ... see—I told you it was easy to get in a mess! So I'll avoid much of this meta-discussion. To introduce her theory it suffices to say how it differs from two common broad approaches to the subject.

One general viewpoint is found mainly in philosophy, which tends to think of concepts in the first place as the constituents of thought. For example, the thought that dogs bark contains the concepts DOG and BARKING. Another strand of this view is to think of concepts referentially, as pointing to or picking out some thing or things in the world. This allows a distinction to be drawn between what a concept refers to and what a thinker in practice applies it to. For example, DOG refers to all and only members of the canine species, so a person is wrong if they think THAT'S A DOG on seeing a fox. That is, the referential approach insists that there is a distinction between how a thinker in fact uses one of his concepts and what would be a correct use. Just thinking that foxes are dogs needn't mean that your DOG concept includes foxes. There is an immediate parallel here with our discussion of intentionality. There, we saw that causal-informational theories of content have unintuitive consequences because they allow everything that causes a representation to form part of the referent of that representation. That objection to causal/informational theories relies on the same distinction: that there is a gap between what a concept applies to and how it is, in fact, used. In short, one broad way of thinking about concepts is as referential thought constituents.

The second tendency is the exact opposite: to think of concepts primarily as the way people actually categorize things. This is more common amongst psychologists, because they usually study the ways that experimental subjects in fact react to things and sort them into categories. They obtain data on patterns of categorical judgment and then formulate theories about the mental machinery that best explains these data. One influential version holds that humans store prototypes of very many categories. These prototypes represent features which are typical, but not definitive, of members of the category. The process of categorizing some encountered item is then thought to involve finding the prototype with which it has the closest match.

Millikan's work on concepts, as you would expect, takes an original direction. Her approach has something in common with both of the foregoing viewpoints. Her theory concerns just one type of concept: empirical concepts of "substances." She is with the philosophers in thinking that concepts *refer*, in a way that may differ from how they are

Concepts

actually applied. Millikan argues that concepts should be individuated not in terms of what a thinker actually applies them to, but instead by what the concept is supposed to apply to. She explicates such purposes in terms of evolutionary functions. But she differs from the philosophical approach in that she does not think of concepts, in the first instance, in abstract terms as thought constituents. Rather, her starting point is that concepts are practical abilities to keep track of things. The model is the way that a thinker identifies another person, and then keeps track of him. This perspective makes contact with the psychologists' interest in studying actual behavior, although she differs radically from them in being concerned with what a person is supposed to identify or track, rather than how they actually categorize or classify the items they encounter. Unlike the psychologists' means of categorization, the referent of Millikan's concepts will come apart from a person's discriminatory dispositions, since the referent is determined by evolutionary functions. That is a virtue of her theory. She takes the means of categorization studied by psychologists as of interest only in elucidating the fallible methods people actually employ to keep track of the underlying referent of a concept. So Millikan eschews the philosophical starting point of concepts as thought constituents, and thinks of them instead as abilities to identify or track some underlying substance. Nevertheless, she can perhaps connect with that role for concepts, if her concepts can be thought of as combining in thoughts like *dogs bark*, each constituent concept somehow contributing to the completed thought.

To make use of the idea that there are things in the world that concepts are supposed to apply to, Millikan relies robustly on the existence of real kinds. Her tactic is to abstract away from the myriad of individual differences in means of categorization by observing that a thinker's identificatory abilities should "cut nature at its joints." She relies on those joints to draw referential boundaries between her concepts. So her theory needs a strong realism about the existence of real or natural kinds, independently of thinkers. Millikan takes her first task to be to explain how this can be so, by developing the idea of "substances"—the things in the world that many of our concepts refer to. We will start there too.

4.2 Substances

Millikan's discussion of substances argues for the existence of a multiplicity of real categories in the world, independently of thinkers. It does not concern concepts directly. Rather it is a piece of metaphysics setting out how the world is. Millikan will need this structure in order to explain how concepts can play their referential role.

In ordinary meaning "substance" covers things like gold, water, and clay—undifferentiated portions of material with uniform properties. Millikan uses substance as a term of art, deriving very roughly from Aristotle. Her usage gives it a much broader meaning, "substance" being something like the material bearer of properties. Millikan's substances include things like individuals and species, as well as material stuffs. Three typical examples are: *Mother, milk,* and *mouse*. Individuals are a paradigm case: my mother, say, who I can reidentify, and who keeps many of her properties as she moves through time and space. Individuals needn't be people; this teacup on my desk is an individual. The main idea is that natural kinds are to be seen as being basically like individuals. As a starting point we can think of a substance being anything that stably bears a variety of properties.

For example, *cat* has properties which are true of every member of the species: warm-blooded, furry, etc. There are also special properties for each individual cat that carry over from one encounter to subsequent encounters: size, color, normal habitat. So if you come across a cat that is 14 inches long, ginger colored, and domesticated, it is very likely that when you encounter that same individual again it will be about 14 inches long, still ginger colored, and living in somebody's home. The key feature of Millikan's substances is that a variety of properties project from one encounter with the substance to another. The cat example shows the two main ways properties can project. Some properties will be true of any instance of the substance, like being warm blooded for the substance *cat*. Other properties will vary amongst individuals, but will be stably true of the same individual: like the size and color of an individual cat. So it is a higher-order property of the substance *cat* that the size and color of individual cats can usually be projected from occasion to occasion. Contrast chameleons, for which color does not project, even for individuals; and ant colonies, for which size does not project. The property projections need not be perfectly reliable. For example, the property of *having a tail* is true of most cats, but does not extend to them all. Projection of such reliable properties is part of what makes a substance, even if there are exceptions.

Although the co-projectability of properties is the core of the idea of a substance, there is a further constraint, which is that the properties should be co-projectable for a single reason. Millikan calls this reason the *ground* of the substance. Chemical elements are archetypal

Concepts

substances, and very many of their properties project from occasion to occasion, such as color, melting point, valence, conductivity, etc. The single ground underlying the projectability of all of these properties is that portions of a given chemical element all have the same inner structure: they are all made of atoms with the same atomic number (number of protons in the nucleus). This underlying ground explains why properties like the melting point and valence of potassium, say, project from any sample of potassium anywhere in the world to any other sample of potassium. It is not only atomic number, but many different kinds of inner nature that can ground the co-projectability of properties, and hence the existence of a substance. Other examples include: diamonds, which all consist of the same crystal structure; stars, which have the same types of unfolding nuclear reactions; and suspension bridges, which all distribute and balance loads in a similar structural pattern.

Millikan's substances also include items that are similar because they have a common essence that does not derive from their inner nature. Her example is geodes, the often colorful crystal deposits treasured by mineral collectors. Geodes vary enormously, but they all share some features, like the fact that they are roughly oval arrangements of crystals around a central core. These similarities arise from the fact that all geodes are formed by the same natural forces out of similar material in similar circumstances. That type of similarity can also ground the co-projectability of the properties in a substance.

The second main type of substance is not grounded in a common essence, but rather in historical relations. The model is biological species. The members of a species need have no inner nature in common, although they may. What is definitive of the similarity between members of a species is the fact that they are descended from a common ancestor. The phenotypic traits of each member of the species are inherited from this common ancestor, and this shared inheritance grounds many dimensions of similarity. It will not necessarily make them the same size as one another, but it will give them the same skeletal arrangement and reproductive methods, for example. The projectability of properties across instances of these historically-based substances is ultimately founded in copying from one generation into the next. It is like explaining why all the copies of a photocopied handout have a smudge in the top right-hand corner, on the basis that the original had a smudge in the same place. In the case of species, in addition to brute copying underlying co-projectability, there are other forces at work: shared traits may have been selected in similar historical environments to perform common biological functions.

Individuals are an important type of Millikan substance. Take an individual person. Many of her properties are projectable from occasion to occasion, across a broad range of properties that we make use of all the time: things like her height, appearance, preferences, character dispositions, and so on. The reason that such properties are stably true of the same person can be thought of in two ways. First, the same person at different times is very similar in her internal structure and these similarities underlie the projectability. But in living organisms there is another reason, more akin to historical substances. That is the operation of the homeostatic mechanisms that keep us alive. If the lifetime of a person is thought of as a series of brief time-slices, each causing the next, then it is the copying of one person time-slice into the next, under control of homeostatic mechanisms, that ensures the projectability of properties from one encounter with a person to another. Inorganic objects can be thought of in the same way: as a series of time-slices, the structure of one time-slice causing similarities in the next.

Millikan can be pluralistic about what grounds the co-projectability of properties over her substances, but it is crucial that there be such grounds, because she needs her substances to have a real existence in nature. The ground gives a Millikan-substance this real existence. Not any old case where properties happen to co-occur will do. A substance is real just in case, in relation to each pair of instances of the substance, there is a single principle that explains why they are alike in a number of respects.

Millikan calls the information about what kinds of properties are projectable over instances of a given substance a *template* for that substance. So the substance template for *cat* says that size and color are projectable over different encounters with the same particular cat, and that things like type of metabolism (in the cat: warm-blooded) projects across the entire substance. On the other hand, a property like shape does not project. Cats can be found curled up in a ball or stretched out like a log. Think of a substance template as a questionnaire with a series of blanks to be filled in. The blanks represent properties that will project, and once their values are ascertained these values will project across the substance. So the substance template for a new species X has blanks like: Method of reproduction? Habitat? Method of locomotion? Metabolism? Examining a sample X fills in these blanks and the values project across all other Xs. Notice there are two kinds of blanks. The first are for things which, once ascertained, will be true of all instances of the substance. The melting point of copper is an example. The

Concepts

second are properties that do not project across all instances of a substance but which, for that kind of substance, are stably true of an individual instance, and project across encounters with that individual. For example, cars vary widely in size, but the size of an individual car remains fixed from encounter to encounter. Contrast this with tidal estuaries, whose size varies from encounter to encounter. Conversely, the location of an estuary does not vary, whereas an individual car moves around and cannot be counted on to be in the same place from occasion to occasion (in inner London this is true no matter how well you lock up your car).

Human thinking with substance concepts makes powerful use of substance templates. Millikan illustrates this with the concept AFRICAN DORMOUSE. Although you are unlikely to have encountered that concept before, by applying your substance template for mammals you will know what kinds of properties will project across instances of the substance *African dormouse.*

The idea of these substance templates is not that they are part of the substance itself, but rather that the structure associated with substances allows people to employ substance templates in their thinking, forming an important part of the usefulness of substance concepts.

Substance templates can cover a class of substances. For example, each biological species has similar blanks in its template. So a single template can be applied to all substances that are species. Substances often form a hierarchy of kinds: individual, species, genus, family, order, etc. Where there is such a hierarchy a substance template can be thought of as a concept of some superordinate substance. Just as it is a deep feature of the world that substances nest into superordinate and subordinate levels, it is a fundamental feature of substance concepts that they form hierarchies, allowing the productive use of substance templates.

Substance concepts are useful precisely because not all of a substance's properties are apparent on each encounter with that substance. A substance concept allows the thinker, on encountering a substance, to infer from past occasions the existence of properties which might be useful on the current occasion. (This would be unnecessary if all a substance's properties were openly and readily identifiable.) The usefulness of substance concepts in human thinking also depends upon the properties which co-project being relevant to us. As well as the relevance of a substance's various properties, there are three separate dimensions along which a concept of a substance may be more or less useful in human thinking. The first is the reliability of the property inductions: the more likely it is that a given property of an instance of the substance projects to other instances, the more useful that substance concept will be. The second dimension is the number and variety of possible inductions. The more properties that project, and the more widely varied are the types of properties that project, the more useful the substance concept is. Third, the existence of a well-characterized substance template makes substance concepts falling under that template more useful. Each of these dimensions may vary independently to make some substance concepts more or less useful than others, depending upon the context of use. For example, even if a substance only supports very rough and tentative property projections, a concept of it may be useful if the substance supports a large number and variety of such rough projections. Correlatively, a substance that supports a small number of highly reliable property projections may be of little use if that is all that can be projected. We can think of those substances, concepts of which are useful for humans, as being useful substances. But remember that whether or not a substance exists does not depend upon how good or bad a concept of it is for our purposes, but simply upon whether there exists a real ground for the co-projection of properties across instances.

To summarize, a strongly realist ontology of substances is the first plank in Millikan's theory of concepts. It is needed in order to make compatible the referential and categorical roles that concepts must play in any theory of human cognition.

4.3 The Place of Substances in Psychology

Millikan's metaphysics of substances is neither plucked out of the air nor is it distilled from philosophical writings stretching back to Aristotle. It is a view arrived at by philosophical reflection, but also receives empirical support, because if the world is full of the substances that Millikan describes we would expect them to be important for human interests. Millikan's primary claim about human psychology is that the metaphysical importance of substances is reflected in the wealth of human concepts that are concepts of substances. But she also relies on evidence about the development of infants and children. She argues that concepts of substances appear very early in conceptual development. This is an area where the experiments are notoriously open to alternative explanations, so Millikan's reading of the evidence cannot be taken as established scientific fact. However, she does at least show that her substances are compatible with empirical work on conceptual development.

Millikan argues that substances are the sorts of things that infants begin to track perceptually before being able to predicate any properties them. So when a very young infant follows the trajectory of an object as it goes behind a screen and emerges on the other side he is tracking the individual physical object, which is a substance. By doing so he can come to learn which properties of physical objects remain constant over time. So he starts with a perceptual concept, which he can use to start tracking things in more conceptual ways: *toy, food,* etc. The important developmental claim is that infants start keeping track of a substance without first identifying or having any concepts of properties of the substance. There is no process in the infant equivalent to the chain of reasoning: that is moving thus and so, so it must be a physical object. The order of explanation goes the other way round. Being able to track substances allows infants to learn about their properties. Substances must initially be reidentified using mechanisms that do not employ any prior concepts. Only when a child has lots of concepts up and running will prior concepts be employed in the recognition of some substances. For example, it is a more sophisticated operation to reason: furry, purring, domesticated, therefore cat; than it is just to reidentify a cat, say, by responding to a furry feel and purring sound with the thought CAT on various occasions.

Millikan's evidence is drawn not only from how infants track objects, but also from what young children say about substances. There is a lot of research that suggests that children tacitly believe that there are principles underlying the unity of a substance, even though they don't know what those principles are. This is evidence that children from an early age assume there are grounds for property projection, well before anything is known about what those grounds might be. Millikan also relies on evidence of early grammatical distinctions. One thing distinctive of substances is that they can be referred to by subject-place terms in sentences. For example, in "dogs bark" the term in subject position, "dog," refers to a substance whereas the predicate only refers to a simple property, *barking*. (Recall from the last chapter that predicates often refer to properties, and it is of the essence of predicates to admit of negation; thus, properties have contraries.) Properties like *barking* do not have the rich structure of grounded co-projectable properties possessed by substances like *dog*. (Millikan agrees, however, that the distinction between substance and property is not absolute. A substance may also be a property.) Terms for substances can be marked as singular or plural, and with the definite or indefinite article, showing that they are more than just ways of talking about properties.

The distinction between the different psychological roles of concepts of substances and of properties also does some important philosophical work. If substances were always identified via properties then there would be a question how we ever manage to identify properties in the first place, leading to a potential regress. Millikan relies on the empirical literature to motivate the claim that concepts of substances are basic and that identifying a substance need not proceed by preexisting grasp of any of its properties. A substance concept can merely be practical, exercised in knowing how to use things. Practical concepts of substances can thus form part of the theory of how we come to have concepts of properties. Predicating properties of a substance is more sophisticated than tracking it practically, since it requires a grasp of the concept of negation, for the reasons discussed in section 3.4 of the last chapter. Millikan is also able to avoid the trap of assuming that thinkers using a substance concept must have knowledge (explicit or tacit) of criteria of identity for that substance. It is part of her theory that we do not, in general, operate with criteria of identity when tracking a substance, but only with some means of identification that manages to track the substance well enough for some purpose.

4.4 Against Conceptions

Concepts are individuated by the substances they have been designed to track or pick out. Section 4.5 will establish that, for each concept, there is a real substance that it is supposed to refer to—the thing which the thinker's categorical ability is designed to track in that instance. The current section undertakes an important preliminary task: to distinguish concepts from conceptions. Conceptions are the ways that a thinker actually manages to track a given substance. So conceptions may be highly idiosyncratic. They are the means of categorization studied by psychologists, because they are the ways that thinkers actually apply their thoughts to things in the world. It is a distinctive virtue of Millikan's theory that she so forcefully rejects the idea that conceptions have any role to play in fixing the reference of a concept.

To see the distinction, consider two people who knew president John F. Kennedy: his daughter Caroline, and an ordinary voter. The voter will identify President Kennedy by properties like his political party, his TV appearance, his policies, etc. Kennedy's daughter will use some of the same means of identification, like her father's appearance, but will rely on much more personal cues, like his voice, his posture, etc. The two have quite different conceptions associated with their respective concepts of John F. Kennedy—their means of identifying differ in many ways. But on Millikan's theory they nevertheless have the same concept, because they have a concept of the very same substance, namely Kennedy, the person. Her theory also allows people to be systematically mistaken about the descriptions they apply to some concept. For example, lightning was thought in ancient times to be caused by the gods. On Millikan's view the ancients had the same substance concept as we do; they were referring to the very same kind of electrical discharge, but they were just systematically mistaken in some of their beliefs about it. In fact, there are still widespread mistaken beliefs about lightning; most people think that it emanates from clouds, whereas, in fact, electrons usually travel from the ground up. Millikan's view says why the meteorologist who knows the facts and the ordinary person with their mistaken conceptions can be referring to the very same substance, *lightning*. Conceptions need not be explicit knowledge, but may just show up as tacit assumptions in the way that a concept is used, for example, in recognizing a substance.

It is very common for theorists to take a person's concept to refer to all and only those things that person would categorize under that concept. That would be to take the conceptions that a thinker associates with a concept as definitive of the extension of that concept. It is a very natural way to think about concepts, explicitly formulated in much philosophical literature, but also underlying most psychological writing about concepts. The assumption is motivated by what Millikan calls *meaning rationalism,* the view—or hope—that the meanings of our terms should be readily available to us as users of these terms. Within the domain of concepts the meaning rationalist assumes that what fixes the reference of a person's concepts is the ways they actually apply it—that is, the conceptions associated with the concept. To undermine explicit and tacit meaning rationalism, Millikan makes a robust assault on the idea that conceptions have any role to play in determining the reference of a concept.

Millikan's stance requires her to reject any theory that equates a concept with a thinker's associated descriptions or methods of perceptual recognition. This puts her in good company, because attempts in both philosophy and psychology to formulate description-based theories of concepts have met with widespread failure. The history of philosophy is littered with inadequate attempts to define terms like justice, virtue, knowledge, and beauty. Psychology has not done much better, finding little evidence that people operate with defining descriptions even for such simple concepts as DOG. It is only in highly formalized domains like mathematics that it is at all plausible that descriptions define a concept.

Millikan does not deny that we can have concepts that determine their extensions by description, although they are rare. She calls these classifiers. But they are not substance concepts. A concept X may work as a classifier if it is taken to apply strictly only to items that have some set of properties, A, B, C, and provided that classifying an item under concept X does not lead the thinker to infer anything beyond its possessing properties A, B, and C. For example, I may sort my books into fiction, science, mathematics, and philosophy books, and further divide them up by nationality and gender of the author. I can have a concept X that just applies to those books on my shelf written by American female philosophers. But the fact that a book falls under concept X tells me no more than that it is a philosophy book by an American woman. Concept X is then a pure classifier and not a substance concept. A concept may be a pure classifier because there is no underlying substance to which it could refer. In addition, it could be that some concepts work as classifiers even though there is a substance that their descriptions, in fact, pick out. A concept would be a classifier, even if it happens to pick out a substance, provided its associated description is taken to fix the reference of the concept, rather than being just a means of identifying the referent. It is doubtful that there many such concepts, for reasons we will see below.

Substance concepts are part of a productive system of information storage and use. Once I can identify a substance, I can continue to learn more about its projectable properties, and I can also learn ways to identify it more accurately and in a greater range of circumstances. The identifications are productive. I don't use the fact that humans have two kidneys as part of my means of identifying people, but on seeing my own x-ray and learning that I have two, I can instantly project that new property to most other people I encounter. This productive use of substance concepts does not require sharp boundaries between substances. Nor does it rely upon any agreement between different people's means of identifying a substance (their conceptions of that substance).

By contrast, a scheme of pure classification requires for its effectiveness sharp boundaries, drawn by defining descriptions. To be any use, everyone operating with the classifier must employ the same conception. Such schemes are effective for storage, retrieval, and

Concepts

transfer of information. Examples include the way books are classified in a library and the way goods are classified in an automated product-ordering system. We saw earlier that Millikan's substance concepts are means of identifying and keeping track of some substance. Notice that classifiers work the opposite way around from identifiers. The properties of the object must be ascertained prior to classifying it, whereas a substance can sometimes be identified before any properties are predicated of it, where the thinker has a purely practical concept, knowing how to keep track of the substance and what to do with it. Millikan argues that most of our concepts are closer to identifiers than classifiers, because a classification system is necessarily limited. The knowledge that some object x is classified as X contains only as much information as is analytically put into the class: it tells you that x has the properties definitive of X and nothing more. In order to learn more, the thinker must either examine the object or treat it as a substance of some sort, to make grounded inferences to further properties.

The distinction in public language between words that function as classifiers and identifiers is not sharp. Some switch over time from classifier to identifier, and back, so that it may not be clear which role is being played. For example, in trying to understand some group of medical problems a term may be introduced as a classifier, listing a series of criteria needed to qualify for the syndrome. This syndrome can then be the object of further study and often, once more is understood of its underlying nature, the initial definition is revised. It then becomes a substance term, properties of the disease being projectable in virtue of some underlying mechanism. At this stage typically some of the properties definitive of the original syndrome are rejected because of the subsequent understanding of the underlying mechanism. In such cases there is a gray area between the term being used as a classifier and as an identifier. The term starts as a classifier, both because of ignorance about the underlying mechanism, and because some convention is needed to facilitate medical discourse—the standardized definition allows people to communicate about the same "thing," where the thing is just shorthand for the set of definitions. Knowledge of the underlying mechanism allows the term to become used as an identifier: if an underlying substance is discovered there is no need for the anchor of a conventional definition. Millikan accepts that the distinction between terms that function as classifiers and identifiers is one of degree, but argues that the latter kind of terms express more significant concepts.

The idea that our kind of terms are mostly classifiers is also undermined independently by a long-standing philosophical argument. In an influential paper in the 1950s, W. V. Quine rejected the idea that there is a rigid distinction between analytic and synthetic truths. Analytic truths are made true by the definitions of the terms they contain. Synthetic truths are true because of the way the world is. Quine marshaled influential arguments to the effect that an absolute distinction between the analytic and the synthetic was unsustainable. That is grist to Millikan's mill, because it implies that no term can be determined in advance to remain forever a classifier—that would require strict, analytic ties to the properties definitive of that term.

Millikan is not alone in expressing skepticism about the power of an individual's conceptions to determine the content of concepts. Other theories make the same move—using the objective reality of certain categories in the world as part of the machinery of reference determination. On one type of view typified by Hilary Putnam, thinkers' conceptions of a natural kind leave some leeway as to what the essential nature of that natural kind actually is. For example, people think of water as the transparent, colorless, odorless, potable liquid around here, but many different compounds could have turned out to be playing that role. Water happens to be almost entirely hydrogen dioxide (H_2O), consisting of the lightest isotope of hydrogen, but it could equally have been made up of deuterium dioxide, or perhaps some other compound. Putnam's view is that thinkers' conceptions do some of the work of drawing boundaries, but the natural kinds actually found in the world have an ineliminable role to play in determining reference. Millikan's view is much more radical than this. Her substances do not just take up the slack left over by people's conceptions. Rather, real substances determine concept identity, and conceptions have no role to play, except as a description of the idiosyncratic means that different thinkers happen to use to identify a given substance.

Another type of philosophical view eschews reliance on an individual's conceptions in determining reference, in exchange for relying upon common conceptions shared within a thinker's linguistic community. A typical proponent is Tyler Burge. The reference of a concept is fixed by conceptions, but an individual must often defer to experts, or to the majority view within his community, as to what are the conceptions determinative of the reference of his own concepts. Burge's view is that a thinker's reference to the extension of one of these concepts "goes through" the conceptions out in wider society. Where Burge's view relies on conceptions from outside of the individual thinker to determine what the individual is thinking,

Concepts

Millikan's theory relies only on the reality of substances. That is a virtue of her theory, but it seems to limit her ability to deal with concepts that are closely tied up with societal practices. In my view, however, Millikan's theory can incorporate the society-based cases, because she can allow what I will call *societal substances*. Societal substances are ones where the ground for co-projection of properties lies in the practices or traditions of a community. Marriage is a good example. A whole range of properties can be roughly projected of married people: they cohabit with another married person of the opposite sex, they often wear rings, etc. The ground for these co-projections lies in the social expectations and legal obligations underlying the category. So the law decides what is to count as being married, and when it comes to an end, and enforces various covenants. Society adds to this a myriad of expectations, traditions, and obligations; all of which actually cause the properties of marriage to be roughly projectable. However, there is nothing in this case like the internal essence of a chemical element. The real-world grounds of societal substances are people-dependent.

Societal substances serve to blur the distinction between concept and conception, since the ground of societal substances lies in the community's collective conceptions. The distinction made by Millikan remains good, since the individual's conceptions do not logically determine the reference of his concept; but conceptions cannot be excluded entirely from reference-determination, because they come in again in explaining causally the grounds underlying the existence of the substance. In practice there is a continuum from concepts of substances that are grounded entirely in mind-independent facts, like the substances treated by the natural sciences, to rougher substance concepts grounded in a community's collective conceptions, like those studied by social science or poetry, say. Millikan's theory was conceived for the more scientific end of the spectrum, and that is where it is most easily understood and applied. However, she also extends it to societal substances, where the way people think actually causes certain properties to be co-projectable.

I should emphasize that in rejecting conceptions as determining the extensions of concepts, Millikan departs radically from the philosophical consensus. Recall that on Millikan's view there is nothing more to having an adequate concept than having the ability to identify a substance in some circumstance or other. And there is no requirement that thinkers share the conceptions under which they think of the same substance. In general they will not. Thinkers count as having the same concept just in case they have abilities to recognize the same substance, whether there is any overlap in their means of identifying that substance or not. This stance rejects a very influential philosophical position, deriving from Frege (who we met in section 3.4), which holds that there is more to sharing concepts than just referring to the same thing in the world. In Frege's view thinkers also share some of the information they associate with a concept, what he calls a concept's "sense." There is not scope here to explore this deep issue, but it should be flagged. Translated into Millikan's terminology, Frege gives us strong philosophical reasons for supposing, contrary to Millikan's view, that there is something stable at the level of conceptions shared by thinkers—a Fregean sense—in addition to the reference of their concepts. Millikan argues vigorously that thinkers do not in general share Fregean senses (or anything like them), and that psychological explanation does not need to assume that they do. She holds that almost all psychological explanation should proceed via concepts individuated at the level of reference. Concepts of what I have called societal substances may help to make this stance more palatable. But it remains a difficult position to defend. It is often a good philosophical technique to adopt a radical position in order to get to the heart of its pros and cons. The second half of *On Clear and Confused Ideas* does so. It consists of a brave attack on Fregean senses, together with an explanation of how Millikan's theory accounts for the various psychological roles usually played by senses. She does allow that some psychological explanations advert to an individual's particular conceptions, but she vehemently denies that there is anything intersubjectively stable at the level of conceptions, nor anything remotely like Fregean sense. It is a difficult project and Millikan makes significant progress. It is worth reading the book to see Millikan's radical approach worked out in its details, and to judge for yourself whether she succeeds.

4.5 Concepts as Abilities

So much for the rejection of conceptions as determinative of reference. What then does determine the reference of a concept? To answer that we need to examine more closely what Millikan's concepts are. A widespread assumption is that concepts are like words: they are symbols in the head. Millikan rejects that view, at least as a starting point. For her, concepts are abilities to identify and reidentify. So a substance concept is an ability to identify some substance. Abilities are quite a different kind of thing than internal symbols, so Millikan's view is a major departure from philosophical orthodoxy. However, it fits well with psychological research since, as we have seen, experimenters study what people do in applying concepts, and Millikan too starts from people's practical abilities. There is a big difference, though. Whereas psychologists study actual discriminatory practice, including mistaken applications of a concept, Millikan uses the term "ability" to idealize away from a person's dispositions to categorize. Instead, she counts abilities by what it is their purpose to identify. An ability can be supposed to identify substance X, despite the fact that the set of dispositions that realise that ability sometimes fail to identify X and sometimes misidentify other substances as being X. So the key features of the theory are: (1) concepts are abilities; (2) abilities are individuated by their natural purposes; (3) a concept refers to that which is the purpose of the ability to identify; and (4) a thinker realizes that ability through some set of associated conceptions (actual dispositions to categorize), but these are not determinative of reference.

Millikan's unorthodox ontology that counts concepts as abilities can easily be reconciled with concepts as symbol-types. In her view, an ability to identify a substance will always be mediated by some internal representation, since she is liberal about what count as representations: they need not be word-like elements in a language of thought. If we sort mental representations into types depending upon which substance they serve to identify, then for each representation type there will be an associated substance concept. Therefore, in such cases concepts can be thought of as mental representation types. The subtle difference in ontology (abilities vs. symbol types) will make little difference to the theory. (This means of reconciliation needs some modification to deal with redundant concepts, which are discussed later in this section.)

Millikan's theory of what an ability is designed to identify is, unsurprisingly, Darwinian. This makes the terminology potentially misleading. In Millikan's theory, possessing an "ability" to identify substance X does not imply that the thinker is in fact able to identify X in any actual circumstances. Rather, it means that the mechanism was selected in the past for identifying X. It will follow that the thinker is still able to identify X if those historical circumstances recur, as usually they will. More carefully: an ability to recognize X implies that the person has a disposition to identify X if they try to identify X under the conditions that accounted for their past successes in identifying X; where trying to identify X is the initiation and running to the point of success or failure of a mechanism or program designed to identify X.

Concepts

But a change in environmental circumstances can leave a thinker with a mechanism the purpose of which is to identify substance X, but without any current means of doing so. That is not a difficulty for Millikan's theory, but it must always be remembered that "abilities" are counted by their ends, not by the means of identifying, and so do not depend on what a person can actually do.

How does this theory of concepts square with Millikan's teleosemantic theory of the content of representations? An ability to identify looks at first like an input-oriented notion. Does it run counter to Millikan's forward-looking theory of content, with its fruitful focus on outputs as determinative of content? In my view, it does not. The forward-looking nature of teleosemantics is reflected in Millikan's insistence that actual dispositions to categorize do not determine the reference of a concept. Instead, abilities are individuated by what it is their natural purpose to identify. But what is a "natural purpose to identify"? It is like a natural purpose to represent. Recall that there was a potential problem with teleosemantics' claim that the content of a representation is what it is the natural purpose of that representation to represent. The problem was the unexplained use of "represent." The problem was solved by teleosemantics' forward-looking approach: a representation is supposed to represent that state of affairs that is an evolutionary condition for the successful performance of the evolutionary function of the mechanism which consumes that representation. So teleosemantics reduces the idea of "a natural purpose to represent" to unproblematic physical facts (that do not contain the notion of representation). In exactly the same way, teleosemantics reduces a "purpose to identify" to evolutionary conditions for the successful performance of the evolutionary function of some consumer mechanism. And Millikan's abilities are purposes to identify. So they are forward-looking after all. In sum, the connection between teleosemantics and the theory of concepts is that the former is needed to naturalize the terms used in the latter (i.e., abilities to identify and natural purposes to identify).

Many of our human abilities to identify were not selected in our historical past, but are instead learned in an individual's lifetime. Thus, just as Millikan's teleosemantic theory had to place considerable reliance on derived evolutionary functions (section 3.3), here too the theory of concepts must rely upon derived purposes. Where a new ability to identify is arrived at by learning, its purpose comes not from some selectional history, but from the purpose of the learning mechanism. For example, dogs can learn to recognize each other by their scents. When a dog smells a new scent, it stores some olfactory trace that enables it to tell when it comes across the same scent again. Each new scent encountered thus becomes the basis of a new ability to identify. What are the purposes of these abilities? Let's suppose that the learning mechanism was selected because it enabled dogs to keep track of other individuals by means of their unique smells. Then the purpose of the learning mechanism is to produce new abilities to recognize individual conspecifics by their smell. Thus, in considering Rover's scent-based ability to recognize Canina we are justified in saying that the purpose of that particular mechanism in that individual dog is to identify *Canina*—that is its end, what it is meant to do. The purpose derives from the selectional evolutionary purpose of the learning mechanism.

Most human abilities to identify substances will have these kind of derived purposes. So the full theory allows that an ability to identify has its purpose in one of two ways. Either it was selected to identify substance X, or it was produced by a mechanism that was selected to be tuned to identify substances *like* X, that has actually been tuned in this case to identify X. The "like" here is doing a lot of work. It means that the mechanism is operating in the same manner and according to the same principles as accounted for past successes of the learning mechanism. The upshot is that there need be no encounters with substance X in the organism's selectional history (there may have been no dog in history with a scent quite like the distinctive smell of Canina) provided that the organism learns to identify X using the same mechanism operating by the same principles as accounted for learning to identify other similar substances in the evolutionary past.

According to Millikan's theory, there are lots of ways in which an ability may fail to operate as it is supposed to. These are thus various sorts of failure of the concept. The most basic sort of failure was discussed in the last section: a person's conceptions will not normally perfectly reflect that which it is the purpose of their substance concept to identify. It is a great merit of Millikan's theory that it explains so clearly how reference determination differs from actual means of identifying (psychologists' "categorization"). So the theory allows that some person may stably misidentify cows as horses whenever she encounters them on a dark night. Nevertheless, her concept retains its reference to horses, and only to horses, if its purpose is to identify horses. That is, Millikan's theory of concepts uses teleosemantics to solve the disjunction problem about the reference of concepts.

The second kind of conceptual failure is equivocation. A person may acquire some new ability to identify in a confused way, so that it points simultaneously to two substances. In that case, the concept will refer equivocally to both. Suppose the purpose of a relational mechanism in newborn infants is to enable the infant to learn to recognize its food-giver by sight and smell, and then to react by preparing for feeding. What if by chance the infant picks up a visual trace of its father in addition to the olfactory trace of its mother? Then the new person-recognizing system will be equivocal between its mother and its father. So the concept will refer to the disjunction of the two substances: Mom-or-Dad. (Careful: the infant's equivocal concept does not have the internal structure of the disjunctive concept I have used to express it; rather it is a single concept with a disjunction at the level of content.) More radical confusion on acquisition will lead to the third kind of conceptual error, reference failure. There may be just no fact of the matter about what some new mechanism is supposed to identify. In such cases the person has a quasi-concept that fails to refer, because there is no substance that is it the purpose of the ability to identify.

Finally, Millikan's theory allows for conceptual redundancy, an important kind of failure in a person's conceptual system. Redundancy arises where a thinker has two different mechanisms the purpose of each of which happens to be to identify the very same substance. In that case the person has two mechanisms that he treats as abilities to recognize different substances, but which in fact are supposed to recognize the very same thing. Each ability will carry different means of identifying the substance, but the thinker could greatly enhance his range of property projections were he to realize that the conceptions associated with one concept could also be employed in the other. Here is a classic philosophical example of the phenomenon. A person could have known the author Mark Twain through his writings and some famous biographical information, while also knowing the very same man by sight (under the name Samuel Clemens) as his next-door neighbour in Connecticut, without knowing that the two conceptions were of the same individual. Such a person would have two substance concepts referring to the same individual, since we suppose that each ability was supposed to track that individual. By keeping the two identificatory mechanisms distinct, the thinker retains a redundancy in his conceptual system. In this way, although Millikan counts abilities by ends, she can make sense of the fact that thinkers sometimes keep two mechanisms separate, which are in fact abilities to recognize the very same substance.

Redundancy is remedied by a thinker putting together the two sets of conceptions and treating them as means of identifying the same substance. Then the two mechanisms are no longer separate. Conversely, a thinker might mistakenly treat as the same two different concepts. Equivocation will result. Suppose, in my gross ignorance (i.e., I don't know Mark Twain is dead), I mistakenly arrive at the conclusion that my current reclusive Connecticut neighbour is Mark Twain. Before merging the concepts, I had two abilities, one to recognize my neighbor, Grumpy Fred, and the other to keep track of information about Mark Twain. After merging, there is no single individual which my ability can be said to track. It equivocates between Mark Twain and Grumpy Fred. So the mechanism for remedying redundancy will lead to equivocation when misapplied.

Equivocation and redundancy are relatively common conceptual failures. However, we do have ways of guarding against them. Equivocation will typically show up when errors of identification correlate systematically with conception sets. Going back to the infant's equivocal concept of Mom-or-Dad, he will fail whenever he attempts to suckle following visual identification, and succeed when identifying by smell. The tacit inference from *It's X* to *Suckle!*, where X is the equivocal concept Mom-or-Dad, fails systematically when X is identified under the visual conception, and succeeds systematically when X is identified under the olfactory conception. This kind of correlation of failure with means of identifying is a revealing sign of conceptual equivocation. And it is the kind of thing we guard against in our conceptual abilities. Correlatively, redundancy will show up in the accumulation of coincident conceptions attached to two substance concepts treated as different, and the absence of contradictory conceptions.

In sum, Millikan's innovative idea is a fruitful theoretical tool: many empirical concepts can be treated as abilities to identify and keep track of substances.

4.6 Substance Concepts through Language

Humans' use of language gives us a particularly powerful way of forming new concepts. Many theories take linguistically-based concepts either to be the foundation of all conceptual abilities, or at least to be a special case. By contrast Millikan argues that recognizing a substance through a linguistic label is no different in principle from recognizing it by any other means. She says that the shout "Hey guys, it's raining!" is just as much a sound of rain as is the pitter-patter of drops on the roof. The important idea is that language sounds can carry information in the same way that, say, light can.

Millikan relies on some psychological evidence for her position. Experiments suggest that under circumstances of high task-demands (e.g., because of speed constraints or distractions) things that we are told are directly stored as beliefs, in exactly the same way as things that we perceive are. So, she argues, identifying a substance by a public language word is just like tracking it by any other perceptual means.

This allows us to acquire new concepts with remarkably thin resources. All you need is a word for a new substance together with some idea of the relevant questions to ask about it (a rough substance template). The concept of African dormouse that I offered to you earlier is an example. The substance template for mammals will tell you what kind of properties you should learn about the substance, on the basis of what is likely to be projectable. The word alone acts as a seed crystal around which a richer conception of the substance can grow. You can recognize the same substance again just by the fact that other speakers use the same word for it.

Acting in this way, language hands us, for free, abilities to recognize substances we have never encountered. I may never have met the British Prime Minister, but his name allows me to collect together lots of different bits of information about the same person, e.g., he looks like that face on TV, he wears glasses, etc. Each of these conceptions would help me to identify him if I encountered him. Knowing how to recognize the same name again is a means of recognizing him: it is a conception of him. Even without encountering him the name acts as a focus marking the fact that all the conceptions should be organized together into a single means of identification, because they are all about the same individual. In this way language allows us to form concepts of things that no longer exist, such as people who are long dead. No one may now be able to identify Alexander the Great in person, but his name acts as a means for unifying lots of pieces of information as all being about the same man. This allows Millikan's theory to explain how your and my concept of Alexander the Great are both abilities to identify that man, even though he is long dead.

So a person can acquire a new substance concept just by applying an appropriate substance template to a word used to name the substance. Often template and identifying ability must be acquired separately: you won't acquire the concept of BREET unless I also tell you that it is a person's name, say. However, sometimes the word alone

Concepts

will tell us which substance template to use, because of society's stable conventions about naming substances. For example, the suffix *-ium* on a word usually indicates that it refers to a chemical element that is a metal. So if you did not already have it, you could get the concept VANADIUM from the word alone (in the context of an appropriate sentence).

It is a controversial idea that, to identify a substance, it is enough to be able to recognize a public language word. However, if correct, it is an enormously powerful way to reconcile language-first and thought-first theories of concepts.

5
Local Natural Information

5.1 The Relevance of Information

Natural selection cares only about effects. Therefore, Millikan's theory of intentionality is forward-looking (chapters 2 and 3). Consumer systems read representations so as to select behaviors, and content derives from the evolutionary conditions for successful performance of those behaviors. Recall, however, that the producer system is also implicated, because it is an evolutionary condition for the performance of all of its evolutionary functions that the representations it produces correspond to the world. The consumer reads representations according to some assumed correspondence between different representations and worldly conditions; the producer's purpose is to generate representations when the conditions given by that correspondence actually obtain.

How does the producer do that? How can it tell? Intuitively, representation producers use perceptual mechanisms that pick up on regularities in the environment. They rely on things in nature that signal the states of affairs of interest, in the way smoke signal the presence of fire. For example, the bacterium's magnetosome is sensitive to the local magnetic field and takes it as a sign of the direction of oxygen-free water which, in the Northern Hemisphere, it is. The signs needn't be perfect, but there must be some correlation between sign and signified. Stimulations arriving at the sense organs carry all sorts of information, in the sense that if you were a detective, you could use these sensations, together with appropriate hypotheses and background assumptions, to infer very many things about the world outside. Some sensations would lead to sure conclusions and others would merely raise the probability of some state of affairs above bare chance. But the situation of an organism in the wild is similar to a code-breaker in a war: even a slightly increased probability can be important knowledge when the stakes are high enough.

The basic concept is as follows: whenever there is a correlation between two types of things, sign and signified, the sign is said to carry *information* about the signified. Millikan rejects the idea that information can form the basis of a naturalization of intentionality. However, even her teleosemantic theory needs there to be information in the environment that can be used by representation producers. In recent work she has explained what kind of information is needed.

The same worry about how production mechanisms can do their job arises from the theory of concepts in chapter 4. Substance concepts are abilities to track substances. But how can an organism do that? Again the answer must involve relying upon some kind of correlations found in the environment. As Millikan says:

> It is only because there is much natural information in the world to be mined that it is possible for an organism to manufacture intentional representations.

What is this "information"? Millikan's theory of *local natural information* is what is needed to explain how representation producers and substance trackers can do their job. The theory introduces local natural information as a theoretical term; and then explains why it is found in the natural world, and how it is used by organisms to produce representations and track substances.

5.2 Local Natural Information

Millikan's starting point is Fred Dretske's careful work on information. The basic idea is that a sign carries information in virtue of being correlated with what it signifies. Dretske deploys a strong definition requiring, given some background circumstances, the signal always to coincide with what it signs as a matter of exceptionless law; so that the occurrence of the sign implies the existence of the signified. In this sense, for example, the colored light emitted by street lamps is a sign of hot sodium gas. That spectrum of emitted light raises the probability that sodium is present to certainty. Millikan argues that this concept of information ("law-information") is too strong. The information needed by perceptual mechanisms is weaker and more common. Her idea is that a sign carries local natural information whenever it correlates with some environmental feature, but that correlation need only extend through some local domain, and may not be globally applicable. Furthermore, all correlations count, not just those which raise the probability of what is signified to certainty. (Occurrence of the sign makes the feature signified more likely, but that probability may be less than 1). The only constraint argued for by Millikan is that the correlation should extend through some local domain for a single reason: there should be some univocal account of why a correlation found in one part of the local domain continues to other parts. For example, in reacting to a moving shadow and diving underground a mouse is making use of local natural information. The shadow carries the local information that there is a predator overhead, although there is no strict-law connection or conditional probability of 1 between the two. Millikan's central insight is that, in order to produce representations, and to identify substances, psychological mechanisms can make use of this more common local information, and not just Dretske's rarer law-information.

There are actually three reasons why something weaker than law-information is still useful to organisms. The first we have just seen—the sign may serve only to increase the probability of what it signifies: the shadow on the ground might be a predator, and that is good enough for the mouse.

Second, a particular sign-signified correlation may only hold within a limited geographical area or for a restricted period of time—mist on the north Welsh coast indicates imminent rain; exactly the same kind of mist, when found on the desert coast of Namibia, carries no such hope. So there is no correlation as a matter of universal law, but still a correlation that is useful in identifying within a particular domain. This may be partly catered for within Dretske's law-information by means of his "channel conditions," the conditions that must be satisfied for there to be a strict correlation between sign and signified. Being in a particular geographical area might be one of the channel conditions. But there is a logical problem here: the sign can never simultaneously carry information about the signified and carry the information that its channel conditions are satisfied—something cannot both be a sure sign of some signified and simultaneously be a sure sign that all the background conditions are satisfied that are needed to make it a sure sign of the signified. So channel conditions have to be presupposed by the thinker at some stage, without any basis in law-information, on pain of regress. Thus, the satisfaction of channel conditions is just like actually falling within some appropriate local domain: the organism need not be able to tell when it falls within that domain.

The third consideration makes a very important and much neglected philosophical point: since laws are necessarily general, there can be no laws about individuals as such. Laws can deal in properties that happen to apply to an individual, but will not discern between one individual and its duplicate with the same properties. Causal interactions are blind to whether individual A or individual B is doing the causing. They depend only on A's and B's causally relevant properties. In the absence of laws treating of individuals, there can be no law-information about individuals. So a theory which bases intentionality in law-information has a problem with representing individuals. Organisms do need to represent and keep track of individuals (starting with their mothers, at least in mammals), and it is pretty clear that they manage to, somehow. How do they do it? By keeping track of grounded correlations concerning individuals, e.g., a face having such-and-such features correlates strongly with the presence of Johnny. Millikan's local information can therefore include information about individuals, where law-information cannot.

In short, the information needed by a representation-producing system may only be chancy: probability-raising; and a sign may only be correlated with what it signifies in some local area. Notice also that a natural sign is only any use if it does actually recur within a domain. One-off co-occurrences are useless, even if they have arisen as a matter of natural law. So Millikan limits her use of "information" to correlations that do actually recur (Dretske's law-information need not). For these reasons, Millikan also calls her theoretical concept "*recurrent local natural signs.*" I will continue to call it local information, for short.

The argument for the usefulness of local information is that natural selection is likely to have designed perceptual and cognitive mechanisms to take advantage of many circumstances where a sign is useful. All this requires is that there is some grounded correlation between sign and signified. That is Millikan's notion of local information: it is carried by signs whose types are correlated with something in the environment (the signified), there being a univocal reason, grounded in natural necessity, why this correlation extends through a period of time or from one part of a locale to another. The correlation need only be strong enough to be useful to natural selection. Whether a correlation is strong enough will depend on what the information is used for. When a mouse mistakes a shadow for a predator there is relatively little cost, compared to the cost of being eaten. So in some domains false positives may be very common, and the sign-signified correlation correspondingly weak. A further merit of Millikan's proposal is that it caters for this variability. Local information is just what she needs.

5.3 Intentionality from Local Natural Information?

So systems are able to produce representations by making use of local information in their environment. This suggests an interesting proposal about intentionality in general. There's lots of information around, but the only systems *designed* to produce information are representation producers: perceptual systems and the like. Conversely, it is plausible that any intentional representation must at least carry local information about what it signifies. Might then intentional representation come to just this: carrying local information for use by some co-operating consumer mechanism as a matter of natural purpose? That would be an interesting way of uniting Millikan's recent theory of local information with the teleosemantics of LTOBC.

Millikan examines this proposal at length in *Varieties of Meaning* (2004). In the end, she concludes that it doesn't quite work. One of the reasons is that representation producers may make use of a whole collection of relatively weak local natural information, producing representations only when enough of the alternative natural signs are present. In such cases there is no *single* reason why the representation, considered as natural sign, coincides with the world. There will be a heterogeneous collection of correlations, each grounded in natural necessity for a different reason, which together explain why the representation is produced so as to coincide with a condition in the world with a probability better than chance. Human recognitional abilities are probably like that: they rely on a collection of correlations and when there are enough present conclude IT'S AN X. Millikan requires that local natural information be grounded in a univocal reason why the correlation continues throughout some domain. Therefore some intentional representations will not count as local natural signs.

Of course, there *is* a single reason why signs generated by a representation-producing system covary with the world. That is because it is an evolutionary condition for the performance of the evolutionary function of the producer system that they should so covary. However, *that* was the reason in which the theory of intentionality was itself grounded. So to expand the concept of local information to include such signs would just be to adopt the theory of intentionality from LTOBC. The terminology is clearer if "local natural information" is reserved for those correlations grounded in reasons other than having been selected to represent. Many intentional representations will carry local natural information. But we are considering a class in which:

(1) the sign coincides with a condition in the world because of a variety of grounded reasons, that is, the producer mechanism runs off a variety of weak correspondences; or

(2) for the correlation to be grounded requires that some prior state conditions are satisfied or that some independent natural uniformities hold.

The intentionality of such signs cannot be reduced to carrying local natural information for use by some consumer mechanism as a matter of natural purpose, since they do not carry local information at all. However, teleology still delivers a determinate content for such signs: they refer to the evolutionary conditions for the successful performance of the function of the consumer mechanism. So the teleosemantics has priority, and local natural information comes in as that which organisms rely on to produce representations.

An alternative view is possible, however. That would be to argue that being selected to represent does qualify as a univocal reason for a grounded correlation between sign (in this case, representation) and signified. Many of the items that do qualify as local natural signs on Millikan's definition will have been selected to coincide with what they signify. Just one example is the pattern on a moth's camouflaged wings, but the phenomenon is extremely widespread. Why then exclude those correspondences that have evolved for representational purposes, and which otherwise would lack a univocal reason for the correlation? The issue is subtle. However, what is clear is that even were Millikan's definition expanded to include such cases, teleology would still be needed to fix the content of representations. The proposal we have been trying out is not that a sign designed to coincide with some condition (for consumption by a consumer mechanism) represents all the things it signifies. The proposal was that a sign represents only that which it is the sign's natural purpose to coincide with. Because of this qualification, the teleosemantics comes in after all to determine reference, however wide the concept of local natural information is drawn.

In short, even if the concept of local natural information is broadened, teleosemantics is still needed to determine reference. However, this is not Millikan's main reason for rejecting information as a naturalization of intentionality. Her primary consideration is that looking at representation from the production end (backward-looking) is the wrong approach. She holds that there can be perfectly good intentional signs that neither carry local natural information nor derive from the scattered evidence of a series of different local natural correlations. Intentional signs can be true merely by accident. For example, a producer system can go wrong and turn out a particular representation when it was not supposed to. Nevertheless, that representation will be read by the consumer system as telling it that some condition in the world obtains. If it happens by accident that the condition does obtain, then the representation is true, regardless of the malfunction of the producer system and consequent failure of the representation to carry any information. Put another way, Millikan's strong intuition is that it is how representations are consumed that determines their content. Therefore, badly-produced representations will still be contentful. Of course, when things proceed as evolution designed them to, production systems will produce representations that carry local information, or at least derive from some conjunction of local correlations. But looking at what happens when things go wrong illustrates where intentionality is really determined.

For convenience, let's use the term "mere intentional sign" to refer to those representations that do not count as local natural signs for the reasons discussed above. Then there is a very interesting parallel between local natural signs and mere intentional signs. They can both be read in exactly the same way. For any mechanism acting on such a sign, it is irrelevant whether it is produced in virtue of some univocally-grounded correlation in the world, or in virtue of the cooperation of lots of different and alternative pieces of local information. This observation gives us a useful way of thinking about things in the world that we humans take to be representations. We read natural signs as if they were representations all the time: e.g., "there's no smoke without fire." These signs do not count as intentional representations because there is no producer system selected to cooperate with us as consumers of that sign in fulfilling some natural purpose. However, if you treat whole human beings as consumer systems, then the teleosemantic means of determining the content of representations can be carried over to natural signs as if they were representations. That is, look for the evolutionary conditions for the successful performance of the evolutionary function (or, more likely, of the derived evolutionary function) of the behavior produced by acting on the natural sign. Those conditions can then be considered as the content of the sign; at least they are what we are taking it to represent on that occasion.

Thinking about natural signs as if they were intentional representations can carry over to language. The content of the signs of written and spoken language is, in principle, determined by the conditions for the successful performance of the functions of the behaviors we produce when people are treated as consumers of those representations. There is an issue whether or not linguistic signs carry local natural information. On the face of it they do not, since their covariance with the world will often be founded in a whole variety of mechanisms. On the other hand, if my proposal about societal substances in chapter 4 is correct (section 4.4) then many words may be signs of societal substances, and if so, the correlation will be sustained for a single reason, albeit one grounded in human intentions and purposes. That is, however, a speculative extension of the basic theory; and an illustration of how Millikan's original ideas open up lots of potential avenues for further enquiry. *Varieties of Meaning* goes on to explore the idea that linguistic signs have to be read in exactly the same way that we read local natural signs.

In summary, the uncontroversial message is that intentional mechanisms produce representations by relying on local natural information in the world. However, there are good reasons why information alone will not do the job of naturalizing intentionality—teleosemantics has an ineliminable role to play in determining content.

6
Externalism

A short introduction to a lifetime of research is necessarily selective. This book only discusses the developments for which Ruth Millikan is best known. It is does not reveal the breadth of her work. By emphasising her facility with empirical science, it underplays the extent to which her views are informed by the history of philosophy, and does not reflect Millikan's important contributions to many longstanding philosophical debates, especially in philosophy of language. For example, part IV of *Language, Thought, and Biological Categories* contains a highly original theory of the logic of negation and identity, explained in naturalistic terms. To give a hint of the importance of her work to mainstream philosophy, this final chapter will take a brief look at how her theories bear on a very philosophical debate: externalism in the philosophy of mind.

Millikan is a resolute proponent of externalism—the idea that a person's mental states are not determined just by how things are with that person, but also by how things are in the world, outside his skin. The idea is puzzling at first. Surely my mental states would not be affected if (disturbing nothing about how things are inside me now) you took me to another environment, or changed some facts about my history, leaving my intrinsic properties unchanged. Descartes is the most well-known proponent of understanding the mind wholly "from the inside," with mental properties discoverable by introspection and not dependent in any way on the nature of the thinker's environment. Externalism presents a radical alternative, which holds out the prospect of showing that some of the problems we have in understanding the mind are dead-end consequences of this internalist point of view.

Thus, in the recent history of philosophy it has been intellectually liberating to be able to think about mental properties, like representational content, as partly determined by things outside the thinker. Relaxing the assumption that content is fixed by a person's intrinsic properties has produced extremely fruitful lines of enquiry. This externalist view has been arrived at for a wide variety of reasons, many unconnected with teleosemantics, by philosophers writing both before and after Millikan. The bibliography gives a few starting points from which to explore externalism. It is a view which has been applied to linguistic meanings as well as to the contents of mental representations. Hilary Putnam advanced an influential argument that the meanings of words for natural kinds (e.g., chemical elements and compounds) depend upon how things are in the speaker's environment (cf. section 4.4). Consider the English word "water," which was used for a long time before scientists discovered that the thing it refers to is in fact H_2O. If there had instead been some different stuff in the physical environment with the same observable characteristics as H_2O, it would have turned out that "water" referred to that other compound. (The idea is not that it is a genuine physical possibility that some other compound could look, smell, taste, etc. like H_2O. Rather, the point is that this possibility is consistent with plausible theories of meaning.) Reference is one of the key semantic properties of a word, so in this alternative scenario the meaning of the word "water" would be different. Which all goes to show that the meaning of our word "water" (which *does* refer to H_2O) depends upon the environment too. The fact that "water" refers to H_2O is determined, in part, by the natural kinds that are actually found in our environment. That is Putnam's argument.

Tyler Burge extended the insight, arguing that the meanings of some words also depend upon a speaker's linguistic community (again, see section 4.4). And there are a whole range of other positions in the philosophy of mind that hold that important mental properties are not fixed solely by a person's intrinsic properties.

By and by, this externalist approach starts to seem pretty intuitive. After all, we are in the business of explaining what human beings do in their environments. Most of what we want to understand concerns people's interactions with the things around them: with foodstuffs, shelter, predators, threats, mates, other humans, and so on. So it starts to seem obvious that how we should properly pick out psychological traits will depend upon the environment that the thinker is interacting with, or evolved or developed to interact with. However, the internalist puzzle remains: how does this connect with mental life "from the inside," where what I'm currently thinking and experiencing seems to depend only on how things are with me, from the skin inwards. This takes us back to a problem I mentioned and then put aside right at the very start of the book: the nature of consciousness.

Internalism is most intuitively enticing when we reflect on conscious experience. But perhaps it is a mistake there, too. Despite substantial empirical advances, especially those deriving from the techniques now available to make images of human brain activity, our understanding of consciousness has not profoundly deepened in the nearly four hundred years since Descartes's time. It is still far from clear how to incorporate phenomenal experience, with its ineliminable subjective element, into the explanatory schema of the objective concepts of physical science. It looks as if we need some major theoretical breakthrough in how to think about consciousness in the first place, as well as more experimental data, if we are ever to achieve a satisfactory understanding of the phenomenon. Questioning internalism about consciousness may be a step towards the required paradigm shift. Furthermore, although mental content (the main subject of Millikan's work) and consciousness (which she understandably avoids) are usually investigated separately, it is clear that they must ultimately be related: the contents of thought determined by the correct theory of mental representation must connect with the knowledge we have as subjects of what we are thinking, which arises from consciousness experience. If there are such connections, and if externalism about mental content is on the right track, then we have some reason to relinquish even our most tenacious internalist intuitions.

In the end, the value of these internalist-externalist tensions is that they provide a fruitful way of generating new ways of thinking, and thus of pushing the debate onwards. For what it's worth, I do think that there are good reasons, not based in introspection, why the nature of conscious experience depends only on what is going on inside the organism. Conversely, any successful theory of mental representation is likely, in my view, to have content determination partly dependent on matters outside the thinker. The need to build a bridge between

Externalism

consciousness and content, and to resolve this underlying tension, is a fruitful challenge for theories in both domains.

In summary, a theme that runs through Millikan's work is her externalism about mental properties. Unusually, her externalism is not a starting-point for formulating her theory, as was the thought-experiment about "water" and H_2O for Putnam, but is rather a consequence of it. As a result, her work provides a new perspective on externalism and, with characteristic originality, enriches the theoretical landscape, nourishing the emergence of fruitful new ideas.

Bibliography

Chapters 1–3, Content, Teleosemantics

Millikan has written an introduction to her theory of content in "Biosemantics," *Journal of Philosophy* 86(6) (1989), pp. 281–297 (reprinted in *White Queen Psychology*, see below), and more recently in the entry on "Teleological Theories of Mental Content" in the *Encyclopaedia of Cognition Science* (Macmillan).

A good way into Millikan's thinking is to read the essays in *White Queen Psychology and Other Essays for Alice*, 1993 (Cambridge, Mass: MIT Press). She has described that book as a retrospective introduction to the difficulties of LTOBC. More on the difference between indicative and imperative representations can be found in "Pushmi-pullyu Representations," in James Tomberlin (ed.), *Philosophical Perspectives vol. IX*, 1996 (Atascadero, CA: Ridgeview Publishing).

Language, Thought, and Other Biological Categories ("LTOBC"), 1984 (Cambridge, Mass: MIT Press) remains the canonical statement of Millikan's theory. The book repays the sustained concentration which it demands of the reader.

Chapter 3 of David Papineau's excellent *Philosophical Naturalism*, 1993 (Oxford: Blackwell), gives a concise introduction to a slightly different version of teleosemantics. The rest of the book locates this theory of content in a wider philosophical setting, and is philosophically important and highly readable in equal measure.

An interesting angle on both Millikan's and Papineau's theories is given in "A Continuum of Semantic Optimism" by Peter Godfrey-Smith in *Mental Representation: A Reader*, S. Stich & T. Warfield (eds.), 1994 (Oxford: Blackwell).

Functions in Mind, Carolyn Price, 2001 (Oxford: O.U.P.) is a good, careful, and recent overview of the various teleosemantic theories of content.

Enthusiasts who want more on the particular issue of historically-based externalism in teleosemantics should see the special issue of

Bibliography

Mind & Language on the topic, vol. 11(1), March 1996, especially Millikan, "On Swampkinds," and Karen Neander, "Swampman Meets Swampcow."

Other Views

The paper most responsible for the demise of definitions is W. V. Quine's "Two Dogmas of Empiricism." It is a classic, and still makes compelling reading. It can be found in Quine, *From a Logical Point of View* 1953 (Cambridge, Mass: Harvard), and is reprinted in A. P. Martinich (ed.), *The Philosophy of Language*, 3rd ed. 1996 (Oxford, O.U.P.).

Mental Representation: A Reader (cited above) has contributions from many of the leading proponents of alternative theories of mental content like Fred Dretske, Jerry Fodor, and Dan Dennett. The collection gives an excellent overview of the problem, and is full of further references.

Ch. 4, Concepts

Millikan's theory of concepts is presented in *On Clear and Confused Ideas*, 2000 (Cambridge: C.U.P.).

Concepts: Core Readings, E. Margolis & S. Laurence (eds.), 1999 (Cambridge, Mass: MIT Press) is an indispensable source of key papers on the major theories. The editors' long introduction to that volume is both highly comprehensible, and a definitive philosophical overview of the topic.

Jerry Fodor, *Concepts: Where Cognitive Science Went Wrong*, 1998 (Oxford: O.U.P.) is a good place to go for a worked-out version of an opposing theory. It is slightly polemical, but entertaining and comprehensible to nonphilosophers.

Ch. 5, Information

Millikan, *Varieties of Meaning*, 2004 (MIT Press), chapters 3–7 (Part II), sets out her theory of information. The book is an extended version of her prestigious Jean Nicod lectures at the *C.N.R.S.* in Paris. The appendix to *On Clear and Confused Ideas* (cited above) contains an earlier version of the theory.

The most influential theory of information, and Millikan's touchstone, is Fred Dretske, *Knowledge and the Flow of Information*, 1980 (Cambridge, Mass: MIT Press), part one.

Bibliography

Ch. 6, Externalism

Two classic papers introduce the topic of externalism in the philosophy of mind and language:

Hilary Putnam, "Meaning and Reference," *Journal of Philosophy* 70 (1973), p. 706, reprinted in A. P. Martinich (ed.), *The Philosophy of Language* (cited above).

Tyler Burge, "Individualism and the Mental," in P. French, T. Uehling & H. Wettstein (eds.), *Studies in Metaphysics: Midwest Studies in Philosophy IV*, pp. 72–121 (Minneapolis: Univ. of Minnesota).

Millikan's views can be found in chapters 7 and 8 of *White Queen*: "What is Behavior?" and "The Green Grass Growing All Around"; and in her more recent "Cutting Philosophy of Language Down to Size" in *Philosophy at the New Millennium*, A. O'Hear (ed.) 2001 (Cambridge: C.U.P.).

Jerry Fodor's public conversion from internalist to externalist makes interesting reading and grapples with many of the issues, see: *The Elm and The Expert,* 1994 (Cambridge, Mass: MIT Press).

Other Millikan Material

Millikan has published a wealth of other papers. Particularly recommended are:

"Truth Rules, Hoverflies, and the Kripke-Wittgenstein Paradox," *Philosophical Review* 99(3) (1990), pp. 323–353; reprinted in *White Queen* (cited above).

"Language Conventions Made Simple," *Journal of Philosophy* 45(4) (1998), pp. 161–180.

"Historical Kinds and the Special Sciences," *Philosophical Studies* 95(1-2) (1999), pp. 45–65.

"Biofunctions: Two Paradigms" in R. Cummins, A. Ariew & M. Perlman (eds.), *Functions: New Readings in the Philosophy of Psychology and Biology,* 2002 (Oxford: O.U.P.).

Millikan's important and original account of the way that the logic of identity and negation reflects the natural structure of the world is given in part IV of LTOBC.

For further references, Millikan's website at the University of Connecticut Philosophy Department carries a bibliography, and online versions of several papers.